Kids Around the World Play!

Kids Around the World Play!

The Best Fun and Games from Many Lands

Arlette N. Braman

illustrated by Michele Nidenoff

John Wiley & Sons, Inc.

Illustration copyright © by Michele Nidenoff. All rights reserved

Published by John Wiley & Sons, Inc., New York
Published simultaneously in Canada

Design and production by Navta Associates, Inc.

The publisher and the author have made every reasonable effort to ensure that the experiments and
activities in this book are safe when conducted as instructed but assume no responsibility for any
damage caused or sustained while performing the experiments or activities in the book. Parents,
guardians, and/or teachers should supervise young readers who undertake the experiments and
activities in this book.

ISBN 0-471-40984-7

Printed in the United States of America

10   9   8   7   6   5   4   3   2   1

To Callan and Abigail

Always find time to play!

Contents

Acknowledgments

I would like to thank the following people for their willingness to help me with my research. Ms. Heide Signes, third-grade teacher at the James Michael Curley Elementary School, Jamaica Plain, Massachusetts, for asking students at the school to help me with game ideas; and to the students at James Michael Curley Elementary School for sharing their games with me: Tadesh Dow Inagaki for information about Go; Kaninu Njoroge for Bottle Cap Checkers; Estella Stephens for Children, Children; Sean Shea for information on Curbs; Franchualiz Manso-Peñaloza for information on hand clapping games; Ms. Dore, sixth-grade teacher at the Stroudsburg Intermediate School, Stroudsburg, Pennsylvania, for lending me her students to test the games; Elizabeth Decker, Jill Decker, Callan Braman, and Abigail Braman for their help with game testing; Ms. Fumiko Kondo and Scott Poluhowich for their help with Ishikeri; Tatyana E. Dodonova, Associate Professor, Department of English Philosophy and Translation, St. Petersburg State University, Russia, for enlightening me about Russian word games; Larry Bond for connecting me with Tatyana; Judy Nancarrow for her information about Dog and the Bone; Elliott Avedon, Bernie Range, and Tova Fisher of the Elliott Avedon Museum and Archive of Games, University of Waterloo, Ontario, Canada, for their information about the game Mühle; Florence Bottin, Zdzislawa Krukowska, Wanda Szymanska Zak, and Louise Duncan for their help with Polish pronunciations; Janice Visalli for her help with Italian pronunciations; Te Rangikaiwhiria Kemara for providing me with Maori information; Liz Ruckel of the Foreign Language Department at East Stroudsburg University for always helping me out, especially at the last minute; to Dr. Ralph M. Vitello, Dr. R. Squier Ball, Professors Aurora González and Makiko Fukuda, and student Alfredo Garcia from East Stroudsburg University for teaching me various foreign pronunciations; to my mom, Jo Naspinski, for Spanish pronunciation help; to Heide Signes for help with German pronunciations; Mark Sherman from the International String Figure Association; Arthur Obermayer for Rubik's Cube information; the Chinese Embassy, Washington, D.C.; the South African Embassy, Washington, D.C.; Dean Milano, Product Development Coordinator, Revell-Monogram LLC, for information on model cars; Kate Bradford, my editor, for all her valuable suggestions; Michelle Whelan for her help with editing; Lia Pelosi and her production staff for brining all the pieces together; James Masters, from *The Online Guide to Traditional Games,* for his help with board games; Kishor Gordhandas for his willingness to help with information about card games from India; and to Emil Signes, Avis Neary, Richard Signes, Bill Serow, and Joyce Wetlesen for answering my questions and lending me artifacts. And last, a big thanks to Larry Kelly, who never lets me down with his support and Web search help.

A Message to Kids of All Cultures

What better way to learn about a culture than through its games and toys? This book will help you get to know something about people from different lands as you make and play with games and toys from around the globe. Through a culture's play, we can come to understand how the people of that culture enjoy themselves, how they spend time together, and how they use things from their environment to create simple yet entertaining games. One thing I hope you discover in this book is that while many of these games and toys are similar from culture to culture, each bears a special identity that makes it unique. Many of the activities in *Kids Around the World Play!* are fun for the entire family. I hope this book will satisfy the kid in all of us and remind us to take some time to play and have fun.

Note: The Web sites mentioned in this book were current at the time of printing. However, Web sites change frequently. To find new ones, do a search for kids' games using a search engine, such as Google at www.google.com.

PART ONE

Tease Your Brain

Brainteasers are some of the most fun, and sometimes the most frustrating, games you can play. Some involve words and others are about math or shapes, but all brainteasers challenge your brain and make you think. Sometimes the game is timed and you have to think fast. When the brainteaser involves having to remember something and remember it fast, it can be tough.

In England, children play a party game by looking at a tray filled with objects, then writing down as many as they can remember after the tray is covered. In South Africa, kids test their memories by looking at drawings scratched in the dirt, then turning around and answering questions about the drawing without looking at it. How do you think you would do at a game like this? You have one hundred billion neurons in your brain, so put those neurons to good use and get busy with these brainteasers!

Word Games

-RUSSIA-

Word games, such as Hangman, word searches, word scrambles, crossword puzzles, cryptograms, riddles, anagrams, and word-in-a-word, are just a few of the many kinds of games using words. Children in Angola, a country on the west coast of Africa, play a riddle game at night while sitting around a fire. Team one asks team two a riddle. If team two answers incorrectly, team one gets the point. If they answer correctly, they get to ask a riddle, but do not get a point. Only the asking team can score. The game continues until everyone falls asleep! In Scotland, kids play a game called Albert Adams Ate an Alligator. Players take turns going through the alphabet and must make up a sentence of exactly five words that begin with their letter. If someone can't think of a five-word sentence, he or she is out.

In the United States, Hangman is a popular word game. One child has to guess what the mystery word is by guessing its letters. For every wrong letter guessed, another child draws part of a stick man hanging from the gallows. The first child has to guess the word before the stick man is finished. Kids in Russia play a similar version, but without the hanging man.

Games *online*

Check out this word game Web site for online crossword puzzles and more:

www.yahooligans.com/Computers_Games_and_
Online/Online_Games/Word_Games

Here are two Russian word games that will give your brain a workout.

Game HISTORY

Though the crossword puzzle is a popular word game played by people all over the world, it hasn't been around that long. Arthur Wynne invented the first known puzzle, which appeared in the *New York World* newspaper in 1913. He called this game Word-Cross and did not realize the craze this simple game would start. By the mid–1920s, people seemed obsessed with playing these puzzles. They couldn't get enough of them. Doctors warned that the puzzles would harm eyesight and keep people up all night! But people just kept playing, and today the crossword puzzle is as popular as it was more than 85 years ago. You can even play this word game online.

Words from Words

Players: *2*

Object of the game:

To make the greatest number of words in the shortest amount of time.

Here's What You Need

- [ ] 2 pencils
- [ ] a few sheets of paper
- [ ] egg timer, stopwatch, or any type of 2-to-3-minute timer
- [ ] dictionary

Here's What You Do

1 Both players think up a word, preferably a long one, to use for the game. Here are some examples: *pronunciation, spontaneous, limousine, apostrophe,* and *veterinarian.*

2 Players choose one word for the first round. Each player takes a pencil and a sheet of paper. Both players print the one word they chose at the top of their paper.

3 When both players are ready, one player starts the timer, and the game begins. Each player must come up with as many words as possible using only letters from the chosen word before the timer stops.

4 Each player checks the other's list, using the dictionary if necessary. The player with the most correct words wins. (Here are some words you can make from *pronunciation: pro, nun, tin, non, tic, noun, rot, action, run, at.*)

Have you ever heard the expression "Necessity is the mother of invention"? It means that when people have a need for something, someone will invent it. During the **Great Depression** (a time during the 1930s of great economic difficulty in the United States), many people lost everything they had. People needed something to do that would make them feel better. Alfred Mosher Butts came up with a solution. He invented a game that combined crossword puzzles and anagrams with chance. He called it Criss-Cross Words. He created a game board and wooden tiles with hand-printed letters. Alfred studied the front page of the *New York Times* to figure out how many times vowels appeared in words so he could determine how many vowel tiles and how many consonant tiles to make. When he tried to sell his game, manufacturers showed no interest. So, with the help of a friend, he began to manufacture the game in an old schoolhouse in Connecticut. He changed the name of the game to Scrabble, which means "to grope frantically" (and if you've ever played Scrabble you know you are always groping frantically to create the perfect seven-letter word). He sold a few games on his own, but in the early 1950s, everything changed. The president of Macy's department store saw the game while on vacation and ordered them for his store, and the rest is history. Scrabble is one of the world's most popular board games.

Create a Word!

Players: *2*

Object of the game:

To think up new words using letters from another word in the shortest amount of time.

Here's What You Need

- [ ] 2 pencils
- [ ] a few sheets of paper
- [ ] egg timer, stopwatch, or any type of 2-to-3-minute timer
- [ ] dictionary

Here's What You Do

1 Both players take a pencil and a sheet of paper, then think up a word to use for the game. Both players must agree on one word for the game. As an example, we'll use the word *boat*. (The word may have any number of letters. Longer words are more challenging.)

2 Each player writes all of the letters from the word *boat* vertically on his or her paper twice, as shown here, to create four rows.

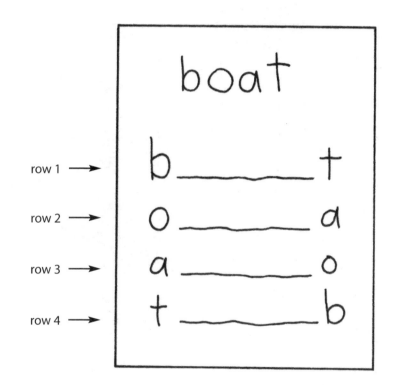

3 When both players are ready, one player starts the timer, and the game begins. Each player must think up words to fill in the blank space between the first and last letter in each row. The blank space in each row may be filled in with any number of letters.

4 The player who fills each blank space in each row with a real word first is the winner. Look up words in the dictionary if you're not sure they are really words or are spelled correctly. (Here are some words from *boat: beet, omega, ago,* and *tub.*)

The Seven Clever Pieces

-CHINA-

A tangram is sometimes called a dissection puzzle because it consists of a solid shape that is cut into pieces (or "dissected"), which are rearranged to create different designs. The Chinese name for tangram is *Chi-Chiao,* which means "the seven clever pieces" because Chinese tangrams have only seven pieces. With so few pieces, you might think these puzzles would be easy to do, but tangrams can be very challenging. Traditionally, the pieces are cut at angles and can be rearranged many ways. The traditional circle tangram is made up of two circles that are dissected with lines and arcs. These pieces are cut out and rearranged to create many different figures with curved edges. Kids all around the world like to challenge their brains trying to figure out how to create specific designs with tangram pieces.

Though we know that the tangram originated in China, not much else is known about its beginnings or who invented it. The earliest Chinese tangram we have is a woodcut from 1780. We also have a book on the subject of tangrams that was published in 1813. But most historians believe that tangrams are probably thousands of years old. Archimedes, the Greek mathematician and inventor who lived during the third century B.C., is said to have created a puzzle, called the Loculus of Archimedes, that earned the name "the puzzle that drives one mad," because of the challenge of trying to use all 14 pieces to create what appeared to be simple designs.

Tangram puzzles were made from ivory, bone, and wood, and some had delicate carvings on the surface. Tangrams brought by people traveling from China to Europe and America became very popular. Inspired by these early tangrams, many people created their own unique tangrams to market and sell. A German company developed the Sphinx puzzle that amused the British soldiers during World War I. American puzzlist Sam Loyd created a challenging puzzle called the Trick Mule

Games *online*

Here are a few Web sites where you can have fun with tangrams:

www.ex.ac.uk/cimt/puzzles/tangrams/tangint.htm
www.enchantedmind.com/tangram//tangram.htm
www.geocities.com/TimesSquare/Arcade/1335/

puzzle, in which the object was to make it look as if jockeys were riding the mules. Today, teachers use tangrams to help teach math concepts. But kids like tangrams because they're fun.

While many kids have seen and played with tangrams containing straight lines and angles, circular tangrams may be a bit easier to do and, when completed, create softer images. After you have mastered the tangrams here, you can create some new designs of your own to try on your friends.

Circular Tangram

Players: *1 or more*

Object of the game:

To create specific designs from given puzzle pieces and make new designs.

Here's What You Need

- 1 sheet of tracing paper, 8½ × 11 inches (21.5 × 28 cm) or similar size
- pencil
- scissors
- 1 sheet of poster paper, such as oak tag, 8 × 12 inches (20 × 30 cm)
- permanent marker, any color

Here's What You Do

1 Place the tracing paper over the tangrams shown here. With the pencil, trace both circular shapes and any lines within the circles. Cut out these shapes.

2 Place each shape, one at a time, on the oak tag and trace the shape using the pencil. Use the marker to draw over the pencil lines. Cut out the shapes. Make sure the shapes fit together well. If any do not, you may need to redraw.

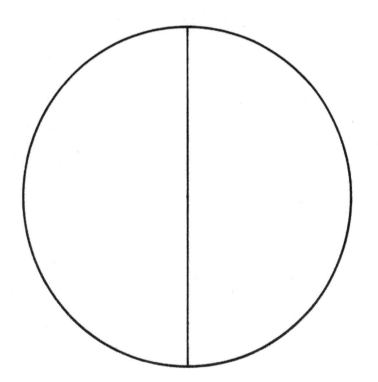

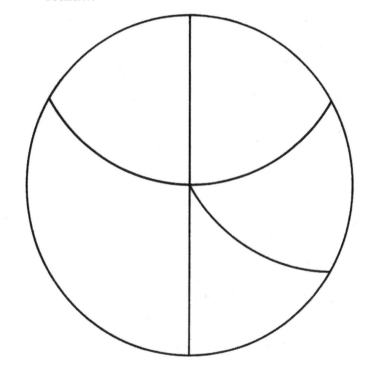

3 If you'd like, you may color in each shape using the marker. Many tangrams are solid colors like black or red. If you color in the shapes, set the pieces aside so the marker ink will dry.

4 Begin by using your tangram pieces to make the designs shown here. (Note: The answers are on page 110.)

5 After you've mastered these, try to create new puzzles to try with your friends, but don't forget to draw copies of each one so you'll have the answers.

Another type of dissection puzzle is the jigsaw puzzle. Most children play with these puzzles today for enjoyment, but the jigsaw actually started out as an educational game in the 1760s. John Spilsbury, a London printmaker, created the first jigsaw puzzle. He printed maps at his shop and mounted them onto thin pieces of wood. Spilsbury then cut the puzzles into large pieces and sold them as a game to help children learn geography. Hoping to gain from Spilsbury's success, other mapmakers began making their own creations. By the early 1800s, English children were using jigsaws to learn about history, religion, and grammar. By the mid-1800s, completing puzzles for pleasure had become the rage. In the early 1900s, when adults began playing with jigsaws, they were faced with a real challenge. At that time the jigsaw box had no picture of the puzzle on the front. People had no idea what the finished puzzle looked like!

Rubik's Cube

Not since 1878 when puzzlist Sam Loyd's famous 14–15 Puzzle hit the market had a puzzle created as much of a worldwide frenzy as the Rubik's Cube did in the late 1970s. Loyd's puzzle contained numbered squares from 1 through 15. All the numbers were in order except 14 and 15, which were reversed. The bottom right space on the board was empty. The player had to slide the numbers around to put them in order. It was difficult to do and drove people mad!

Rubik's Cube had the same effect on people. Everyone became obsessed with trying to solve the mystery of this handheld cube puzzle. People all over the world twiddled with the cube trying to line up the colored squares, often without success. Who was responsible for creating this madness? A Hungarian named Erno Rubik patented the puzzle in 1976, and the Ideal Toy Company manufactured and sold millions of his cubes. But Ideal was sued by a Massachusetts chemist, Larry Nichols, because Nichols had developed a similar cube puzzle and received a patent for it in 1972, four years before Rubik received his. He won his lawsuit, but the cube is still called Rubik's Cube.

Dithwai

Memory games "tease" your brain by letting you have a quick peek at something and then asking you to see if you can remember what you saw. You don't get much time and must quickly memorize something about the object, such as its color, shape, markings, or size. Games like Concentration, in which a player is shown some picture cards briefly and must find the two that match, are excellent memory games.

Games *online*

Here's a cool game you can play online. You get a quick look at a building design, such as a castle, and then you must reconstruct it.

www.kidsnetgames.about.com/kids/kidsnetgames/cs/memorygames/

Many Native Americans from North America played memory games like Concentration using items from their environment, such as stones. In the game Pebble Pattern, the chief of the tribe selected different stones and created a pattern on the ground. Players had about one minute to look at the pattern and then had to recreate the pattern from memory. The player who correctly recreated the pattern first won.

The Sotho people of South Africa play a memory game based on the family traditions of farming and animal herding. The game is called *Dithwai* (pronounced dee-TWYEE), and children need only stones to play. Each player gathers stones with interesting markings, shapes, or colors. Each player builds a "cattle pen" in the dirt and places his or her "cattle"—the stones—in the pen. While one player covers his or her eyes, the other players take cows from the first player's pen and place them in their own pens. The first player must quickly find his or her cows among the other player's cattle. Dithwai is a great game to help build up your memory. The more players you have, the more challenging the game becomes.

Game HISTORY

Dithwai is a useful game for Sotho children to play because they are expected to recognize their family's cattle when the animals are grazing with other families' cattle. Parents believe the skills learned from playing this game will sharpen their children's memory and keep their cattle from accidentally being taken by another family.

Dithwai

Players: *3 or more*

Object of the game:

The player with the most cattle at the end of the game wins.

- [ ] 10 to 15 stones for each player. (Use either stones from outdoors or polished stones from a craft or science store.) Each player should select stones that are similar to each other in color, shape, or markings so that the player can recognize his or her own stones. One player's stones should not look like another player's. However, don't use items like coins for one player and paper clips for another player because this will make the game too easy.

Here's What You Do

1 Each player selects his or her stones and studies the stones, making mental notes about the stones' color and/or markings.

2 Each player builds a cattle pen in the dirt, which is a small mound with a flattened top that measures 2 inches high by about 8 inches long (5 cm × 20 cm). The mounds do not have to be exactly the same, just similar in size.

3 Players decide how many cattle (stones) they will use in the game, and everyone places their cattle on the top, flattened part of their mound.

4 Players decide who goes first. That player must turn around, facing away from the mounds, and close his or her eyes. Each player takes one cow from the first player's pen and places it among his or her own cattle. When they are finished, the players yell, "We capture them!" and the first player turns around to quickly search for his or her cattle. Whichever cattle he or she finds, the player takes them back to his or her mound. If the player misses some, the other player gets to keep the cattle. To make it more exciting, the player who is searching should get about 10 seconds. One of the other players counts to 10 while the first player is searching.

5 The next player to be It is the player in whose pen the first cow was found. Play continues until everyone has had a turn. The player with the most cattle at the end of the game wins.

Culture Link

Twelve Days of Christmas

Most people are familiar with this popular Christmas song. But you probably don't know that it started out as a memory game in England. One player started the game by saying, "On the first day of Christmas, my true love brought to me one ...," and the player filled in a word such as a type of bird. The next player said, "On the second day of Christmas . . . ," filled in two of something, and repeated what the first person had said. The next person did three of something, and so on until players reached the number twelve. Each player had to remember what all of the previous players had added, or he or she had to leave the game. Players definitely had to pay attention to remember everything and repeat it correctly.

PART TWO

Take a Chance!

I n a game of chance you can't control how the game will turn out by using skill, memory, or strategy. Bingo is a game of chance. You have no idea which number the bingo announcer will call next, and whether or not you have that number on your card is only a matter of luck. Games with dice are another example of games of chance. When you throw the dice, any combination of numbers is possible. During the American **Civil War** (between the Northern Union and the Southern Confederacy, from 1861 to 1865), soldiers played dice games such as Birdcage and Chuck-A-Luck and card games such as Seven-Up. With all of these games, the winning soldiers either got a lucky roll of the dice or were dealt a lucky hand of cards.

Games of chance don't always involve cards or dice. Cree children liked to play a game of stick-flipping. Children flipped marked sticks to earn points, never knowing which side of the stick would land face up. Now it's your turn to take a chance playing one of these games.

Gulam Chor

—INDIA—

Gulam Chor (pronounced goo-LAHM chor) is an easy card game played by children in India. The word *Gulam* means Jack, and the word *Chor* means thief. This card game is enjoyed by children in Bombay and in the Indian state of Gujarat. Kids play with a regular deck of cards, but remove one of the Jacks before they begin. Once the cards are dealt, players take turns picking from other players' cards, discarding any pairs they have until someone is left with the unpaired Jack card. That player is the Jack Thief.

Another card game enjoyed in India is *Ganjifa* (pronounced gahn-JEE-fah). It is a traditional Indian card game that may have been played as early as the sixteenth century by royal families. Traditionally, the

cards, made from paper, depict religious pictures and themes with detailed hand-painted designs. A unique feature of the cards is their round shape. Round playing cards are found only in India. The ganjifa cards are handmade. Unfortunately, this art is in danger of dying out. Most of the young people in India are not interested in learning the craft, and there may be fewer than 10 families remaining who make the cards. The black color used on the cards comes from soot, which the artist produces from burning tin with a kerosene lamp. The soot is mixed with **gum** (a sticky plant substance) and is then painted on the card.

The Name GAME

Here's what some card games are called in other countries:

Skat—Germany
Fly—Spain
Rikken—The Netherlands
War—France
Canasta—Uruguay
Cribbage—England

Game HISTORY

The first cards came from Asia and were made from sticks and arrow shafts with markings. These cards were used for **divination** (fortune-telling) long before the seventh century. Stick cards may have been used simultaneously in a number of Asian countries. Historical records mention stick cards with painted pictures being used for card games in China in the seventh and eighth centuries. Later, cards were made from strips of oiled paper. Although European and Asian cards still share some similarities, European cards have developed their own style over the years. French playing cards were the first to use the four suits—spade, heart, club, and diamond—that most people are familiar with today. There are hundreds of card games played all over the world and in every culture.

Gulam Chor is easy to play. All you need are some friends and a deck of cards.

Gulam Chor*

Players: *2 or more*

Object of the game:

To get rid of all your cards by the end of the game and not be left with the lone Jack.

Here's What You Need

- [ ] 1 deck of 52 playing cards

Here's What You Do

1 Before play begins, one person must remove one of the four Jack cards and place it off to the side of the playing area.

2 One player shuffles the deck of cards and **deals** (gives or hands out) the cards face-down one at a time to all the players. Some players may end up with more cards, but that is okay.

3 Each player picks up his or her cards, being careful not to let the other players see the cards. Players pick out any pairs they have and place them facedown on the table in front of them. Number and face cards can be paired; suit cards cannot be paired. If a player has all four of the same card (for example, four 3's), he or she places these cards facedown on the table as two pairs.

4 If a player has three of the same card, he or she may place only two of the cards facedown on the table.

5 When all the players have placed their pairs facedown on the table, play begins. The player to the left of the dealer holds his or her cards in the shape of a fan, and lets the player to his or her left pick one.

This player checks to see if the card he or she selected can be paired up with any in his or her hand. If it can, the pair is placed facedown on the table with the other pairs.

6 The player who just chose a card now fans out his or her cards and lets the player to his or her left pick one of the cards he or she is holding. If the player can pair up the card with one he or she is holding, the card is placed face-down on the table.

7 Play continues in this manner until all of the cards have been paired and discarded. At the end of the game, the player holding the Jack card is the Jack Thief and has lost the game.

Used with permission from Kishor Gordhandas. (Mr. Gordhandas is the largest card collector in Asia with more than 5,000 packs of cards from 70 countries.)

Culture Link
Tarot Cards

Tarot cards were designed in the early 1400s in Italy as a game for the wealthy. Hundreds of years later Frenchman Jean-Baptiste Alliette assigned meanings to the pictures on the cards and they began to be used for fortune-telling. Although the cards remain popular today, they are also considered controversial because of their connection to the **occult** (relating to the supernatural).

Tiu-ü

-CHINA-

Tiu-ü (pronounced TSOOO-you) is a game of Chinese dominoes. Tiu-ü is called fishing because players go fishing for tiles (the domino game pieces) that match the tiles they are holding. There are many varieties of Chinese domino games, but all use tiles with black and red dots. The tiles are rectangular and are made from wood, ivory, or bone.

Dominoes are descendants of dice. Domino games were played in ancient Egypt about 1355 B.C. and also in China in A.D. 1120. The earliest reference to the game being played in Europe is from the middle of the eighteenth century. The popular Chinese game Mah Jong is believed to have developed from the game of dominoes. Kids in Puerto Rico love their version of the game and enter contests and tournaments throughout the state. In Panama both kids and adults play dominoes on their lunch break.

Tiu-ü is one of the easier domino games to learn. You can make your own tiles and play the game by following these directions.

Tiu-ü

Players: *2*

Object of the game:

The player with the highest score is the winner.

Here's What You Need

- 70 craft sticks (Available at craft and discount stores. You'll need only 64 craft sticks for the game, but use the extra ones if you make a mistake.)
- black and red permanent markers

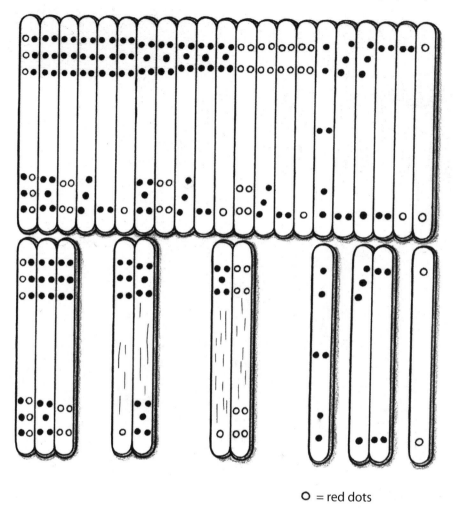

O = red dots

● = black dots

Here's What You Do

1 Make black and red dots on the craft sticks following the patterns shown here. There are 32 sticks shown. You will need to make two sets of the sticks. When you are done, let the ink on the sticks dry.

2 Shuffle the sticks well, then arrange them, facedown, into 16 stacks of four sticks per stack.

3 Take four stacks of sticks from one end of the row and place them faceup in the playing area.

4 Each player takes three stacks from the same row end and looks at his or her sticks. If either player has a pair of double sixes, these sticks are placed on the table faceup in front of the player. No other pairs are removed.

5 On the first player's turn, he or she gets two tries to "go fish." First, he or she tries to match one of the sticks on the table with a stick he or she is holding. If this is possible, the player takes the stick from the table and places it, along with the matching stick, faceup on the table directly in front of him or her. Second, this player now takes one stick from the stack and tries to match it with a stick on the table. If a match is possible, the matching sticks are placed on the table directly in front of him or her. If the stick has no match, the player places the stick on the table faceup with the other sticks in the playing area.

6 The next player takes a turn following the rules in step 5. Play continues in this manner until there are no more stacks of sticks. Players count their scores. Only those sticks the player won by matching are scored. Leftover sticks the player has not been able to match are not counted toward the final score.

Scoring

Large Fish = sticks with 8 or more dots in either color = 2 points for each dot

Minnows = sticks with fewer than 8 dots = 1 point for each red dot only, no points for the black dots. (Minnow scores are always taken to the next 10. So if the total minnow score is 8, it counts as 10. If the total minnow score is 16, it counts as 20.)

The player with the highest score is the winner.

Culture Link

Flower Card Game

Tiu-ü is not the only fishing-type game. In Hawaii, kids play a similar game called Higo Bana. The game is played with cards that have seasonal flowers (iris, wisteria, cherry blossom, peony, and so on) printed on them, one for each month of the year. The object of the game is for a player to match the flower cards he or she is holding with cards that are faceup on the table. Players pick from stacks of cards just as in Tiu-ü. The player with the highest score wins. This game is based on a Japanese flower card game called Hana Fuda.

Le Lotto

Le Lotto, or bingo, is an exciting, edge-of-your-seat game. As the caller announces a number, players frantically search their Le Lotto cards for that number. It might be the one number a player is waiting for. If he or she finds it, that player gets to yell, "Le Lotto!" and wins the game.

This game is played every Saturday night in many cities throughout Italy. People, young and old, gather at meeting halls, fire halls, schools, or church meeting rooms to play the game. Everyone gets a Le Lotto card with rows and columns of numbers, and chips—flat, round disks—to place on the numbers as they are announced by the caller. The caller randomly selects a numbered ball from a container and announces the number to the crowd. If a player has that number, he or she places a chip on the number. When a player has filled a vertical, horizontal, or diagonal row with chips, he or she yells, "Le Lotto," and becomes the winner.

Le Lotto began in the early 1500s in Italy as a state-run lotto, or bingo, game. The game became popular and made its way to France in the 1700s. By the 1800s, the game, with its different variations, had spread throughout Europe. In the early 1900s, people in America started playing the game.

Here's a fun way to play Le Lotto. Use numbers written in Italian!

Game HISTORY

One story about how the lotto came to be called bingo in America goes like this: At a carnival in Georgia a group of people were playing the lotto using beans instead of chips. Edwin Lowe, a toy salesman from New York, stood by watching. When a winner yelled, "Beano!" Lowe liked the idea, so he told his friends in New York about it and set up a game. The winner supposedly yelled, "Bingo!" instead of beano, so he called this new game Lowe's Bingo. In 1930, Lowe hired mathematician Carl Leffler to create the greatest amount of number combinations possible. Leffler created 6,000 bingo cards with nonrepeating numbers. There are some reports that after Leffler finished the job, he went crazy. Today bingo is played on every continent and in 90 percent of the world's countries, using electronic scoreboards and other devices, and is even played over the Internet. But it's still also played the old-fashioned way. In Mexico, for example, children play a bingo-type game with picture cards instead of number cards.

Le Lotto

Players: *3 or more*

Object of the game:

To be the first player to fill a row (horizontally, vertically, or diagonally) with chips.

Here's What You Need

- [ ] 1 24 × 24 inch (61 × 61 cm) sheet of poster board, such as oak tag
- [ ] ruler
- [ ] pencil
- [ ] scissors
- [ ] colored markers
- [ ] plastic bowl
- [ ] chips (use pennies, dried beans, bottle caps, paper clips, or any small items)

Here's What You Do

1 Use the pencil to draw five 5 × 7 inch (12.5 × 18 cm) cards on the poster board. Cut out the cards.

2 Find the **matte** (unshiny) side of each card. Draw 4 vertical lines and 5 horizontal lines on the matte side of each card. The vertical lines should be 1 inch (2.5 cm) apart. The top horizontal line should be 2 inches (5 cm) from the top of the card. The remaining horizontal lines should be 1 inch (2.5 cm) apart, as shown.

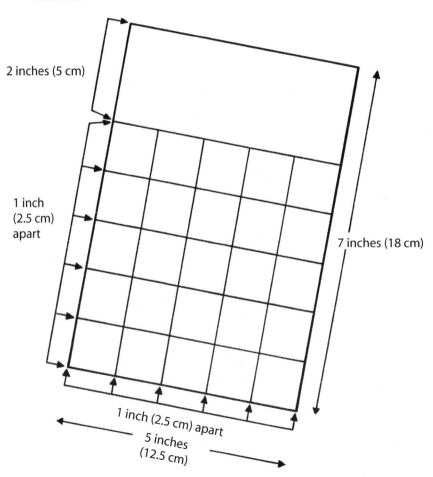

2 inches (5 cm)

1 inch (2.5 cm) apart

7 inches (18 cm)

1 inch (2.5 cm) apart

5 inches (12.5 cm)

3 After you have drawn the lines with the pencil, go over the lines with the colored markers, choosing whichever colors you like.

4 You will be writing the words for the Italian numbers from 1 to 10 on each card. Here's how you write them:

one = *uno* (pronounced OO-nuh)

two = *due* (pronounced DOO-eh)

three = *tre* (pronounced treh)

four = *quattro* (pronounced KWAH-truh)

five = *cinque* (pronounced CHEENG-kweh)

six = *sei* (pronounced say)

seven = *sette* (pronounced SEH-teh)

eight = *otto* (pronounced AU-tuh)

nine = *nove* (pronounced NAW-veh)

ten = *diece* (pronounced DEE-a-chee)

5 Choose any card and write the word "Free" in the center square. Write "Le Lotto" in the top 2-inch (5-cm) section. Then, go to the top left square and write *uno*. In the next square to the right, write *due*. Continue writing the Italian numbers going across

the row, then move to the left side of the next row, and keep writing until you reach *diece*. To fill up the rest of the squares, start with uno again in the next square after *diece*. The first card will end with the number *quattro* as shown.

6 Take a second card and write "Free" in the center square and "Le Lotto" in the top 2-inch (5-cm) section. This time begin with the number *due* in the top left square and keep writing the Italian numbers in the squares until you reach *diece*. Then start with *uno* and keep writing Italian numbers until you reach *diece* again. Continue filling up all the squares with numbers until you reach the last square, which will be *cinque*. (Note: All the cards shouldn't start with the same number. That is why you should start each new card with the next number.)

7 Fill in the numbers on the rest of the "Le Lotto" cards. Write "Free" in the center spaces and "Le Lotto" in the top sections. Start the third card with the number *tre*, the fourth card with the number *quattro*, and the fifth card with the number *cinque*.

8 With the extra poster board, make 10 cards that measure 1½ inch × 1½ inch (4 cm × 4 cm). After you cut out the cards, use the markers to write the numbers *uno* through *diece* on the cards.

9 Decide which player will be the caller. The other players will play the first game. The caller places the number cards in the bowl and mixes

them up well. The other players each take a lotto card and a handful of chips. Each player puts a chip on his or her "Free" square. As the caller picks a number card from the bowl, he or she announces the number in Italian and holds up the card so all players can see the number. If a player has that number, he or she puts a chip on the number every time it appears on the card. The caller puts that number card on the table and doesn't use it again until all the number cards have been announced.

10 Continue playing this way until someone has filled a row horizontally, vertically, or diagonally. When that happens, the player yells, "Le Lotto" and wins the game.

Culture Link

Keno

Keno is a **lottery** (contest in which winners are selected in a random drawing) game that began in China around 2000 B.C. Legend says that a general named Cheung Leung created the game to help bring in money to buy supplies for his men, who were at war with other cities. Players had to pay to play the game, in which they would choose Chinese characters at random on a ticket. If their characters happened to be the ones picked by the people running the game, then they won some money. The rest of the money collected went to support Cheung Leung's army. The game became so successful that funds from the game helped to build the Great Wall of China. The Chinese immigrants who came to America in the nineteenth century to work on the transcontinental railroad brought the game with them.

PART THREE

Sharpen Your Skills

Games of skill require you to be good at physical or mental activities. Dribbling a basketball, having expert aim, running or swimming faster than someone, and thinking up a better strategy are all considered skills. Some people seem to have natural abilities when it comes to particular games of skill. Others need lots of practice to improve their skills. But either way, games of skill are fun to play.

Native Americans and people from other cultures have played a game of skill called shuttlecock for thousands of years. Shuttlecock involves hitting a small object with a tuft of feathers attached back and forth with a paddle. The Native South Americans used a ball made from **maize** (corn) leaves as their shuttlecock. Tibetans played a game of shuttlecock with a ball made from wool. In Japan, shuttlecock is played during New Year's celebrations. Badminton, a modern game of skill that evolved from shuttlecock, may have been first played in India thousands of years ago. Players had to keep an object, or "bird," in the air using a paddle. A net wasn't used until the 1860s. Players not only had to keep the "bird" in the air, but had to get it over the net. The games in this section will definitely sharpen your skills, whether physically or mentally.

Jackstones

—KENYA—

Jackstones is an old game played many different ways by children all around the world. You may already know this game as jacks. Whatever it's called, jackstones is fun to play and requires a bit of skill to play successfully. To play, you scatter your playing pieces, or your jackstones, on the ground, toss a ball in the air, and pick up one, or a few, of your jackstones before the ball bounces on the ground twice. Kids in Kenya play jackstones with stones, but they also use palm nuts, peach or plum pits, and almonds. In the United States, the playing pieces are made from metal or plastic.

Ancient Romans and Greeks called the game knucklebones because the game pieces were made from the anklebones of sheep. Each player threw his or her knucklebones in the air and had to catch them on the back of his or her hand. The player to catch the most knucklebones won. Today, kids play a game called Crazy Bones that is based on the ancient knucklebones game. Crazy Bones has many variations, from tossing the pieces in the air to see how they land to throwing them at a finish line to see which ones land closest to it.

Cultures around the world have used knucklebones for fortune-telling and game playing since ancient times. A mural from Pompeii shows a girl playing a game of knucklebones. Native South American kids use the knucklebones of llamas as their ancestors did. In Ethiopia, children do a little fortune-telling while they play knucklebones. The four sides of the knucklebone are marked to represent the king, the advisor to the king, a peasant, and a slave. A roll of the knucklebone will supposedly determine what the child will be later in life.

Jackstones takes some practice, but in no time you'll play just as well as the kids in Kenya.

Jackstones

Players: *3 or more*

Object of the game:

To scoop up more jackstones than your opponent.

Here's What You Need

- [ ] 15 nuts or pits for each player. (Use nuts in shells such as almonds, hazelnuts, or peanuts, or save pits from peaches or plums, letting them dry for about an hour before using them. If you can't find nuts or pits, use small stones.)
- [ ] small rubber ball (optional)

Here's What You Do

1 Have all players sit in a circle. Each player should place all of his or her jackstones *except one* in a pile in the center of the circle.

2 Decide who goes first.

3 The first player to go tosses his or her jackstone into the air. Using only one hand, the player must scoop up as many jackstones from the pile as possible and catch the falling jackstone with his or her scooping hand. Each player repeats this step on his or her turn.

4 Any player who misses the jackstone he or she has tossed into the air must put back all the jackstones he or she has scooped up.

5 When all of the jackstones have been scooped up, the player with the most jackstones wins the game.

6 This game can be quite challenging. If you cannot catch the pit before it falls to the ground, use the rubber ball. Toss the ball into the air, scoop up as many pits as you can, let the ball bounce once, then catch the ball with either hand.

The Name GAME

What do kids in other countries call jackstones?

Jack Sticks—In Laos, a country in Southeast Asia, children must pick up chopsticks.

Five Stones—In Singapore, a city in Malaysia, also in Southeast Asia, a triangle-shaped cloth bag filled with rice or seeds is tossed in the air while children scoop up stones.

Jacks—Kids in the United States use six-pronged playing pieces, metal or plastic, and a rubber ball.

Truyen-Truyen—In Vietnam, kids pick up chopsticks after throwing a small ball in the air.

Knucklebones—Kids in Iraq use the anklebones of sheep.

Abhadhö

In Tibet, a mountainous country in Asia, children play a similar game called Abhadhö, which means "different ways to grab stones." Players can use fruit pits, animal bones, or stones. This game requires skill because you must first pick up one stone, then two at a time, then three at a time, and so on until you have picked up all of the stones. In Tibet, enjoying the game is more important than winning.

Marbles

−BOLIVIA−

The game of marbles is thousands of years old. The ancient Egyptians and Romans made marbles out of clay and stone. The oldest known Roman marbles date back to 3000 B.C. Children in ancient Rome played the game with nuts and marbles. In North America, engraved marbles have been found in ancient Native American earth mounds. Before marbles were called marbles they were called *bille* (French), *knikkers* (Dutch), bowls or knickers (England), and *marmaros* (Greek). The name *marbles* became the accepted word around the world around the world when marble makers began using marble stone. But when marble became too expensive, china and glass were used. This turned out to be equally costly until the mid-1800s, when a German glassblower invented a tool that would snip off globs of melted glass. This made it much easier to produce the glass marbles. Today, marbles are mass-produced in factories.

Marbles can be played indoors or out-, and it is played in almost all cultures. In Saudia Arabia, players shoot their marbles into three different shallow holes (spaced evenly apart) in the ground. The first player to do this ten times wins. Korean children combine marbles and tag. Each player digs a shallow hole in the ground and marks it as his or hers. From a throwing line, the player must roll the marble into his or her hole. If the player gets the marble in someone else's hole, that player must run to get the marble, then run to tag the other player. If the player tags the other player, he or she gets to keep that player's marble.

To play a competitive game of marbles you need good concentration and a lot of skill. First, you have to learn how to shoot the marble. Some children hold the marble above the other marbles and simply drop the marble. This is the easiest way to shoot. Some

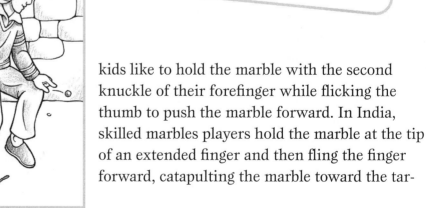

The Name GAME

A marble is a marble is a marble, right? Well, check out some of these marble names:

Boulder: A large marble.

Frosted: A marble that has been dunked in acid to get a frosted look.

Corkscrew: A marble with twists of color running through it.

Milky: An opaque white marble.

Peewee: A tiny marble usually made of steel.

Comic strip: A rare marble that has the picture of a comic strip character printed on the outside.

Swirl: A glass marble with swirls of color on the inside or the outside.

Cat's eye: A swirl marble with a single spiral of color that looks like the eye of a cat.

kids like to hold the marble with the second knuckle of their forefinger while flicking the thumb to push the marble forward. In India, skilled marbles players hold the marble at the tip of an extended finger and then fling the finger forward, catapulting the marble toward the target. In Bolivia, children use their knees to shoot the marble. This method is not an easy one.

Marbles

Players: *2*

Object of the game:

To knock all of your opponent's marbles out of the circle.

Here's What You Need

- stick or sidewalk chalk
- tape measure or ruler
- 10 marbles, 5 in one style or color and 5 in another

Here's What You Do

1 Using the stick, one player draws a circle in the dirt that measures 6 inches (15 cm) in diameter. (If you play on pavement, use the sidewalk chalk.) Measure 3 feet (1 m) from the edge of the circle and draw a line. This is the starting line.

2 Each player takes 5 of the same color or style marble. One player places a marble in the center of the circle. Standing at the starting line, the other player tries to shoot the marble out of the circle. Here's how to do it Bolivian-style. While holding the marble in one hand, place your hand and the marble on your knee and thrust your knee to propel the marble toward the circle.

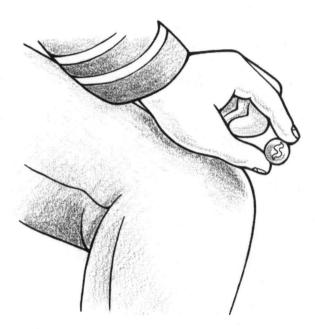

3 If the player knocks the opponent's marble out of the circle, he or she keeps the marble. If the player is not successful, it's the opponent's turn to try and knock the other player's marble out of the circle. Note: If the player's marble did not land in the circle, he or she must put it in the circle before the opponent shoots. Also, if a player knocks the opponent's marble out of the circle and captures it, the opponent must put another marble in the circle.

4 Keep playing until all the marbles are captured. The player who has captured the most marbles wins.

Games *online*

Once you learn to play marbles like the kids in Bolivia, you can try any number of marble games with different rules and strategies. Here are a few Web sites you might want to check out.

www.blocksite.com/wildwood/Ringer.htm (Gives you the rules for the marbles game Ringer.)

www.ehow.com/eHow/eHow/0,1053,3999,FF: (Gives you the basic rules for playing marbles, where you can find cool marbles online, and more.)

www.marbles.net/how.html (Gives instructions on how to organize a marbles tournament.)

www.gameskidsplay.net/games/jacks_and_marbles_etc/marbles.htm (Describes the types of marbles, the basic game, and a variation of the basic game.)

Culture Link
Di-ga-da-yo-s-di

The Cherokee have played a variation of marbles for hundreds of years called Di-ga-da-yo-s-di. It is played on a five-hole course using handmade marbles. Until the early 1900s, players made marbles from chipped stone, which was smoothed into a round shape about the size of a **billiard** ball. (Billiards, which probably originated in France, is a game in which a ball, called a cue, is used to hit three hard balls against one another or against the sides of a rectangular table.) Today, the Cherokee continue to play this game and hold tournaments. Most players use billiard balls, but there are still some traditional marble makers who continue to make the marbles from stone.

Cup and Saucer

String games have existed since prehistoric times. All cultures made some type of string from materials found in the environment, such as strips of hides, parts of plants, grasses, tree bark, and animal hair. In string games, the string was usually twisted and then pulled into various shapes. People who lived by the sea made the string into the shapes of fish and other sea mammals. Desert people made lizards. The Inuit

Game **History**

Many cultures include storytelling with string games. The **Yupik** (the native peoples of western Alaska and northeast Russia) create some of the most elaborate string figures as they tell stories and sing songs. There is a string figure made in Ireland and Scotland called Candle Thief, and a story is told during the game about a thief who steals candles from his neighbor. Strangely enough, thousands of miles away on the island of Papua New Guinea in the South Pacific, a similar string figure is created, but in this story the thief steals pigs!

have a string figure that may represent a woolly mammoth, an animal that lived 10,000 years ago. The Chalupi Indians of Paraguay make a string from cactus fibers and create snake, flower, cactus, and mosquito figures. String games continue to be popular around the world.

Cup and Saucer is a string game that requires concentration and manual dexterity to master. The Cup and Saucer string game comes from New Caledonia, an **archipelago** (a large group of islands) in the southwestern part of the Pacific Ocean. Children in New Caledonia have to watch experienced string artists and must practice many times before they can (successfully) make the different string figures. For many people, string games are a way to pass the time, but for others,

The Name **Game**

Many people remember the string game Cat's Cradle. While one person holds the string figure, the other person picks up the x's in the figure, and transfers the figure to his or her fingers. The game can go on forever. This game has been played in almost every culture. Here are some of the names it goes by.

Woof-Taking—Korea
Woof Pattern String-Taking—Japan
Cradle—England
Taking off Strings—Germany
Cudgi Cudgick—Australia

they are an art form. Some elaborate string figures involve using the hands, feet, and mouth!

Many of the moves in Cup and Saucer are standard moves with many string games.

Cup and Saucer

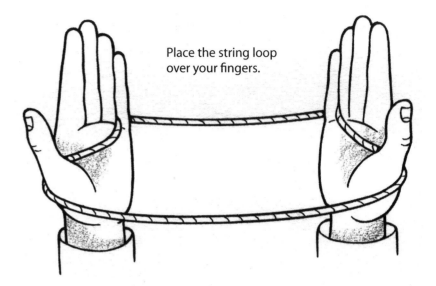

Place the string loop over your fingers.

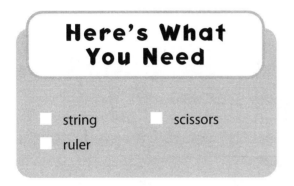

Here's What You Need

☐ string   ☐ scissors
☐ ruler

Here's What You Do

1 Measure a 4-foot (1-m) piece of string and cut it. Tie the two ends of the string in a tight knot. If this seems too long, you can use a shorter piece, but don't use a piece that's shorter than 3 feet (1 m).

2 To begin making the figure, you must learn the first step, Opening A, shown here.

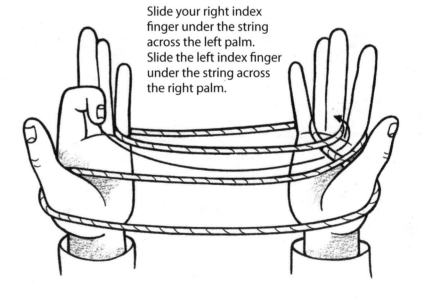

Slide your right index finger under the string across the left palm. Slide the left index finger under the string across the right palm.

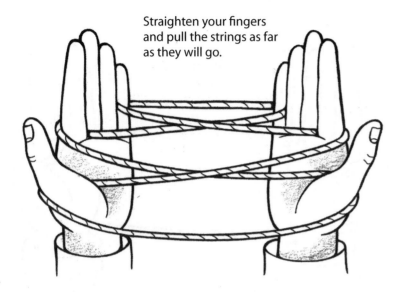

Straighten your fingers and pull the strings as far as they will go.

3 Practice the step a few times until you can do it without looking at the directions.

4 The next step is the sliding-thumbs move. Slide your thumbs under the far index strings and bring your thumbs back toward you as shown.

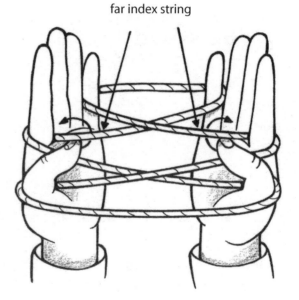

far index string

Slide your thumbs under the far index strings and bring your thumbs back toward you.

Game History

The Navajo move got its name from the Navajo because it's a common move used in many of their string figures. String artist Kathleen Haddon named this move in 1911 because she wanted to draw attention to the people who used it so frequently.

5 Next is another common step called "Navaho the Loop." In this move you lift a lower loop over an upper loop. Since your hands are tied up in strings, it's easier to do this move using your teeth, as shown.

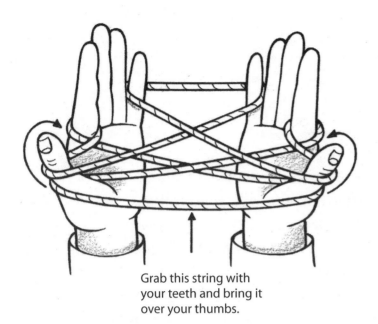

Grab this string with your teeth and bring it over your thumbs.

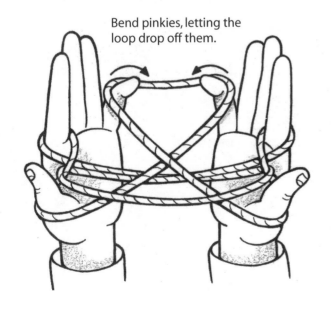

Bend pinkies, letting the loop drop off them.

6 Bend your pinkies so that the loop drops off them, as shown.

Extend hands, pulling strings as far as they will go, and point hands downward.

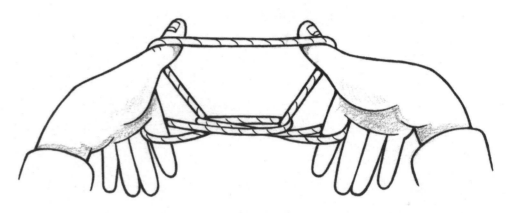

7 Pull out your thumbs to extend the loops and you will see the Cup and Saucer, as shown.

Culture Link

Apache Door

Native Americans have made string figures for thousands of years using materials found in their environment to make the string. The Inuit use **sinew** (a tendon or fibrous tissue that connects muscle to bone) and leather thongs. They also make figures that represent things in their world. They make one figure called the Mouse. The storyteller makes a squeaking sound to imitate a mouse as he or she pulls the strings off the fingers. The Osage make a fishnet called Osage Diamonds, and the Navajo make a Hogan, which is their traditional house. They also make a complicated figure called the Apache Door because it represents the decorated flap of an Apache tent. There are 15 steps in all, and the figure is quite beautiful when completed.

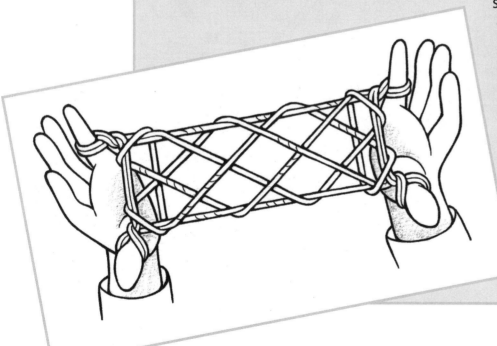

PART FOUR

Ready, Set, Go!

In games that involve a lot of physical action, such as running, jumping, hopping, racing, or swimming, you need to be in good physical shape to compete. Sometimes you also need to be pretty strong.

In Brazil, the Native American children play a racing game in which teams carry heavy logs while running to the finish lines. Strength is also needed for a tug-of-war game that neighboring villages play in Korea. (In tug-of-war, two teams tug on a rope trying to pull the other over a dividing line.) The Koreans believe that the winning tug-of-war team will have a good harvest. In the United States, children, with their legs in potato sacks, race by jumping to the finish line. A similar race game is played in Vietnam with rice sacks. Children everywhere enjoy these types of games because they are competitive and full of action. Get ready, get set, and go enjoy some of these action-packed games with your friends.

Kickball

-MEXICO-

There are all kinds of ball games—football, basketball, baseball, and soccer, to name a few—but kickball is one of the most exciting. You don't need a lot of equipment, but you do need some skill and **agility** (ability to move quickly). Players have to guide the ball through a type of obstacle course using only their feet. The course's twists and turns make it a challenge to get the ball to the finish line. Native Americans from the Pacific Northwest play a game called ball relay. Originally, they used the bladder of a sea mammal filled with air and covered with a woven mesh. Teams formed a line, with players on each team standing about 15 feet (4.5 m) apart. The last player in line had to dribble the ball to the next player in front of him. That player did the same to the next player in front of him until the ball reached the first player in line. That player had to dribble the ball to the finish line. The first player to reach the line won for his team. Today, Native Americans play this game using volleyballs or basketballs.

The students of St. Francis International School in Rome learn the usual subjects such as history and math, but must also learn kickball as part of the curriculum. In Argentina, kids who attend summer camp get to choose kickball from among many other sports. Professional kickball players visit the camps to teach kids better kickball techniques.

Game History

Balls have been part of games for a long time. Women in ancient Egypt threw back and forth a ball made from **papyrus** (a tall, aquatic grasslike plant from northern Africa). Native peoples from the southern-most tip of South America made balls from seal bladders that they filled with feathers. Native North Americans made balls from animal hides, yucca root, mesquite wood, and even volcanic rock. The Choctaw of Mississippi played stickball, the oldest field game in the United States. Today this competitive game is played at the annual Choctaw Indian Fair held each July. Native Americans from **Hispaniola** (an island in the Caribbean made up of the nations of Haiti and the Dominican Republic) used rubber balls in games almost 500 years before Columbus landed on the island.

The *Tarahumara* (pronounced tah-rau-MAH-rah), who live in northern Mexico, are skilled kickball players. Traditionally, they wear one shoe and use their bare foot for kicking. The playing field may cover an area up to 40 miles long. You can understand why their name means "foot runners." Some kids in Mexico like to make the kickball course really challenging. Players have to kick the ball over a log, around a tree, over a tree stump, and under a swing set.

Kickball

Players: *Two teams of 6 or more*

Object of the game:

To complete the course in the shortest amount of time.

Here's What You Need

- 6 rocks (large enough so people can see them) or some other type of marker. (Note: The number of rocks will depend on the number of team players. For 8 players per team, you'll need 8 rocks; for 10 players, 10 rocks; and so on.)
- chalk
- 1 rubber ball about the size of a baseball
- stopwatch

Here's What You Do

1 Decide on the size of your playing area. Choose one end of the area as the starting line and the other end as the finish line.

FINISH HERE

- - - - - PATH OF BALL

START HERE

2 Spread out the rocks or markers in your playing area to create a challenging obstacle course, as shown on page 57. Mark the first rock at the starting line with an S and the last rock at the finish line with an F. Number the remaining rocks from 1 to 4 (or to whatever number of rocks you have) with the chalk.

3 Divide the players into two teams, then decide which team goes first. The first team to take its turn positions its players near the rocks on the course, with one player at the finish line rock holding the stopwatch and another player at the starting line rock with the ball.

4 When the player with the stop-watch starts timing, he or she shouts "Go!" and the player from Team One at the starting line rock kicks the ball toward the first rock. The player nearest the first rock must guide the ball around the rock, then kick the ball toward the player at the second rock. The player nearest the second rock must guide the ball around the rock and kick it to the player at the third rock. This contin-ues until the ball has gone around all the rocks in the course and past the finish line rock. The player with the stopwatch records the time. If the ball doesn't quite reach a rock, the player at that rock may run to the ball and guide it to and around the rock, then kick it to the next rock.

5 Team Two now plays the game following the rules in steps 3 and 4.

6 The team that completes the course in the shortest amount of time wins.

Culture Link

Cane Ball

In Myanmar (formerly known as Burma), a country in Southeast Asia, as well as in China, Japan, and Thailand, kids play an interesting ball game that requires a lot of skill and concentration. It's called cane ball because the ball is made from **cane** (the flexible stem of certain bamboo) and the game dates back to the seventh century. Players must kick the ball to other players on the team using any body part below the knees. The trick is that the ball can never touch the ground! Players learn special ways to kick the ball to keep it in constant motion. If the ball touches the ground, or is taken by the opposing team, the team with the ball loses a point.

Oonch Neech

—PAKISTAN—

Tag is a simple game. One person is It, and must run to catch or tag the other players. But as simple as it is, Tag involves more than just running. You need to be physically fit, agile, and use a bit of strategy to outsmart the player who is It so you don't get tagged.

There are many different types of tag. We know that the Greeks in the second century played a version of Tag. Two teams stood in a line facing each other. One player tossed a shell in the air and the manner in which the shell landed determined which team chased the other. In the Middle Ages, children played Blind Man's Bluff, but called it Hoodman's Blind because whoever was It wore a hood over his or her head instead of a blindfold. The hooded person had to tag players while not being able to see them. In Jamaica, an island country in the Caribbean, kids play Children, Children, in which they chant a rhyme to get the game started. When the children finish chanting the rhyme, the player who is It must run and tag all the players who are the children. From the early 1900s until the 1950s, Tag was popular in the United States and is still played by kids today. American kids also like to play Capture the Flag, in which opposing team members must cross into enemy territory to capture each other's flags without being caught or tagged by the enemy.

The Name GAME

Children everywhere play Tag. There are some interesting names for the game and unique ways to play it.

Hospital Tag—Australia: Wherever the person who is It tags you, you must hold your hand on that spot while you run and try to tag someone else.

The Hunter—Saudia Arabia: The Hunter counts to ten while players hide. Then the hunter must find and tag each player.

Catch the Chicks—Taiwan: One child is the eagle, one is the hen, and the rest are the chicks. The hen tries to protect her chicks from being tagged by the eagle. If a chick is caught, then it becomes the eagle.

Stop—Columbia: Players scatter about while whoever is It tosses a ball in the air and calls someone's name. That child must run back, catch the ball, and say, "Stop." The child takes three giant steps toward the nearest player and tries to tag that player with the ball.

Children in Pakistan play a tag game called Oonch Neech, which means "up and down." One person is It, and must catch and tag the other players. Instead of having one home base where players can run to for safety, the home base can be anything you can jump on, such as a tree stump, a porch, or a chair. As long as you stay on the home base you are safe.

Oonch Neech

Players: *6 or more*

Object of the game:

To avoid getting caught by the person who is It.

Here's What You Do

1 Place the home base objects around your playing area. You might want to use your backyard. If there is a tree stump, use that as well.

2 Decide who is It. The other players stand about 2 feet (1 m) from the player who is It. The player who is It counts to five. On the count of five, the other players run to one of the home bases and jump on top. If the player who is It does not catch or tag anyone, he or she counts to five again. On the count of five, the players must jump off their home base and run to another one.

3 If a player is tagged, he or she becomes It and the game continues until other players are tagged or until everyone gets tired.

Ishikeri

—JAPAN—

Hopping games are found throughout the world. One hopping game, hopscotch, can be played in many different ways, but all hopscotch games include a **diagram** (a drawing showing how something works) drawn on pavement with chalk or scratched into dirt using a stick. To play hopscotch you toss or place a **marker** (an object used as a game piece) inside one of the spaces in the diagram, then you must hop inside the other spaces in the diagram, and back again, before taking back your marker and exiting the diagram. Hopping is usually on one foot. It may sound easy, but this game can be tricky. Your marker must land in a specific space without touching one of the lines and when you hop your foot cannot touch any of the lines. Often only the hand you use to pick up your marker is allowed to touch the ground—the other cannot be used to balance.

In Poland kids play *Klasa* (pronounced KWAH-sah), which means grades in school. The players pretend they are jumping from one grade to the next as they hop through the diagram. Children may choose to use both feet or hop on one foot. Another form of the game is played in Nigeria in western Africa. The diagram used for Nigerian hopscotch is interesting because the parts of the diagram are not connected. Players draw circles in the dirt that are some distance apart. So it's a bit of a challenge to hop from one circle to the next, especially on one foot!

Ishikeri (pronounced ee-she-KEH-dee) is a traditional hopscotch game that children in Japan have played for more than 50 years. In Japanese, *ishi* means "stones" and *keri*

The Name GAME

Here's what kids in other countries call hopscotch.

Pele—Aruba, an island in the Netherlands Antilles
Hop-Round—Great Britain
Gat Fei Gei—People's Republic of China
La Rayuela—Honduras

Game HISTORY

We know that the ancient Romans played hopscotch because one of the oldest known hopscotch diagrams still can be seen. It is etched in a floor in the **Roman Forum** (the great center of Rome where meetings took place). The original hopscotch diagrams may have been as long as 100 feet (30 m). These hopscotch diagrams were used by the Roman army in training exercises to improve soldiers' footwork. When the Romans invaded Britain, British children learned the game from Roman soldiers, who drew the diagrams in the dirt on the roads they were building there.

means "to kick." The game is much like the hopscotch you know, but it gets challenging when certain spaces get "frozen" and players must jump over them to get to other spaces. If three spaces in a row are frozen, it's tough to get to that fourth space without making a mistake.

ishikeri

Players: *Two teams of 5*

Object of the game:

To complete the course without any errors.

Here's What You Need

☐ sidewalk chalk ☐ 10 stones

Here's What You Do

1 Using the sidewalk chalk, draw the diagram outside on the pavement, or in your driveway, as shown below. The diagram should measure about 7 feet, 6 inches × 4

feet 8 inches (2.2 × 1.5 m). For sizes of the inside boxes, see the illustration shown here. Write the numbers in the spaces.

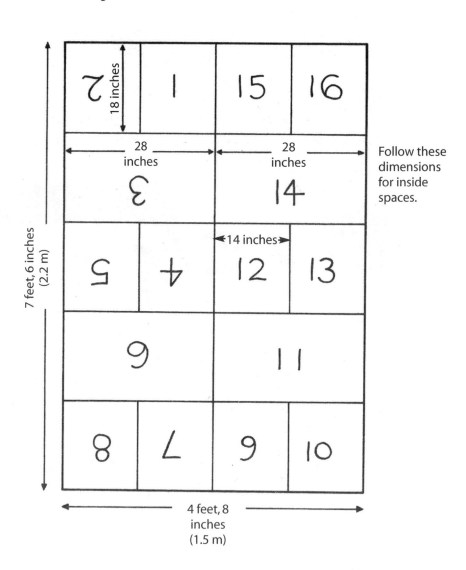

Follow these dimensions for inside spaces.

2 Divide players into two teams. Each player takes one stone.

3 Team One stands in front of spaces 1 and 2, and Team Two stands in front of spaces 9 and 10. One member from Team One drops his or her stone in space 1, which automatically freezes that space, meaning no one is allowed to go in that space until that player has successfully returned to take back the stone. Player one must hop through the diagram starting in space 2, and continuing by the numbers until he or she reach blocks 15 and 16. The player must hop only once in each number space. In the wide blocks, players must hop on

game rules

a. A player may not touch any line with his or her foot.

b. A player may not touch the ground with his or her hand to balance.

c. A player may not put his or her other foot down when there is only a single space. If you break any of these rules you are out and the space your rock is in stays frozen and cannot be used by any players.

one foot only. But when spaces are adjacent, such as a 4–5 or 7–8, the player may use two feet, placing one in each space. At spaces 7–8 and 15–16, the player must spin around and continuing hopping through the diagram until he or she returns to space 2. At space 2 the player will take back the stone in space 1 and exit the diagram.

4 Now it's Team Two's turn. The first Team Two player must follow the rules in step 3 but starts by dropping his or her stone in space 9, freezing that space. Then that player continues on through the diagram starting in space 10, following all the rules, until he or she returns to space 10 to retrieve the stone in space 9.

5 After the player from Team Two has had his or her turn, a new player from Team One goes, dropping his or her stone in space 2, starting in space 1, and continuing through the diagram until he or she exits successfully or is out because of an error. A new player from Team Two goes, dropping his or her stone in space 10, starting in space 9, and continuing through the diagram until he or she exits successfully or is out because of an error. Team members alternate taking turns and continue playing until everyone has had a turn.

6 The game ends when both teams have completed the diagram. The team that gets through the diagram without mistakes wins. If both teams have frozen spaces, the team with the least number of frozen spaces wins.

game rules

a. If a space is frozen, players must jump over that space. If two, three, four, or more spaces are frozen, players must jump over all frozen spaces.

b. Once a player has retrieved his or her stone, that block becomes unfrozen and can be used by other players.

Culture Link

Escargot

French children not only eat *escargot* (pronounced ehs-cahr-goh), which are snails, but play a game called escargot as well. This hopscotch game is called escargot because the diagram is drawn in a spiral resembling the shape of the snail's shell. Children do not use markers in this game, but must hop twice through the spiral to reach the center space and then back out again on one foot. After they complete this task, they may choose one space as a home space, writing their initials in it. That becomes their rest space where both feet may be used. The winner is the child who owns the most number of home spaces.

Flower Relay

—SOUTH KOREA—

A relay is a race between two or more teams, in which each team member participates in only a part of the race and is then relieved by another member of the team. Relay races require team members to work together in order to win. Each player must be ready to do his or her part for the good of the team and give his or her best effort. There is a famous bicycle relay race that starts in the Yukon territory in Canada and ends in Haines, Alaska. Each team member is responsible for biking a specific distance during the race. In Russia, people participate in the Vladivostok relay, a race that starts out with team members driving cars and ends with members sailing boats.

Game History

The Olympics are competitive games that feature athletes from all countries of the world. The men's and women's relay events test the teams' ability to complete a variety of different distance races, including the 400-meter and the 100-meter. Today's Olympics are a modern version of the ancient Greek Olympics, the earliest record of which is from around 824 B.C. in Olympia, Greece. After about 776 B.C., the games were held every four years. Some of the early competitions included foot races, chariot races, boxing, and wrestling. Koroibos, a foot runner, was the first recorded winner. In ancient Greece, only men could participate in the Olympics. Women could face death if they even watched the games. These ancient games remained popular until about A.D. 394. In 1894, Frenchman Pierre de Coubertin worked tirelessly to begin a modern version of the ancient Olympic games. He succeeded and witnessed the first modern Olympic games in Athens in 1896. Today, the Olympics, with a wide variety of events for men and women, are popular worldwide.

Not all relays are so serious. Children all over the world participate in simple relay races because they are fun. The Flower Relay Race, played during festivals in South Korea, is a good example. Two teams compete to see who can decorate two trees with flowers first. It is a fun race and makes the trees look festive for the celebrations. In South Korea, instead of using string to tie their flowers, children usually play this game using trees with thorns. They must attach the flower by pushing the stem onto the thorn. This usually holds the flowers in place, but if a flower falls from the thorn, the team loses. This makes the game more challenging.

Flower Relay

Players: *8 or more*

Object of the game:

The first team to attach all their flowers without allowing any to fall off the tree wins.

Here's What You Need

- [ ] yarn
- [ ] scissors
- [ ] artificial flowers with stems about 12 inches (30 cm) long (available at craft stores, discount department stores, or flower shapes)

Here's What You Do

1 Find two trees outdoors that are not too far apart, with trunks that have about the same **circumference** (distance around the circle). For each player, cut one strand of yarn that measures twice the circumference of the tree trunk. Measure this by wrapping the yarn around the trunk two times.

2 Give each player a flower. Tie the yarn tightly around the stem of the flower at the middle point of the yarn and a little higher than the middle point of the stem.

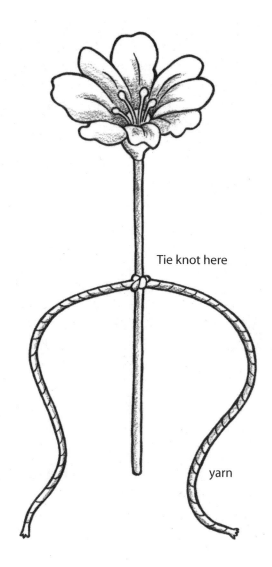

Tie knot here

yarn

3 Divide the players into two teams. Each team selects one of the trees. About 20 feet (6 m) from the trees, the players on each team line up behind one another in two straight lines next to each other facing the trees. Each player must hold his or her flower.

4 When all players are ready, one player yells, "Three, two, one, GO!" On "GO!" the first players in each line run to their trees and quickly tie their flowers around the tree. When finished, they run back to their lines, tap the shoulder of the next person in line, and run to the back of the line.

5 As soon as the next player is tapped, he or she must run to the tree and tie his or her flower to the turn in a different spot. (Flowers shouldn't be tied on top of one another, but may be tied near one another.) That child runs back to the line, taps the shoulder of the next player, and so on until all players have had a turn.

6 The team that finishes first with all flowers attached and the last player tagged up wins.

Twisted Trail

Many Native North Americans participate in relay races. One such race, Kiwa Trail, presented interesting challenges. Players had to race around a difficult obstacle course, having to circle trees that were close together. This game is played today by many Native Americans, but is called Twisted Trail. Markers are set up throughout the course, and the winner is the team whose players circle all of the markers in the shortest period of time. Sometimes markers are placed close together, and at other times, players must circle each marker twice. There is one thing about this relay race that hasn't changed from when it was first played: It definitely will make the player dizzy!

PART FiVE

Never Get "Board"

Although ancient civilizations didn't have cardboard or plastic, they still invented and played "board" games. They simply scratched the game board in dirt or clay, or carved it into stone or wood. All classes of society in all cultures enjoyed board games. Royalty and the upper class played games with carved boards and game pieces, while the peasants played with dirt ones. For game pieces, people used everything from the bones of animals to seeds and pebbles.

Today, there are hundreds of board games for sale. Trivial Pursuit® tests your knowledge of odd facts. Players race around a board earning pie slices by answering questions on different topics, then race home once they've collected them all. Risk is a classic strategy game in which players march their pieces across the globe hoping to dominate the world. Clue, a whodunit game, has been around for more than fifty years. Each player becomes a detective in a murder case trying to figure out three important pieces of information: the killer, the murder weapon, and the location of the crime. The famous game of Monopoly almost never made it to the toy store shelves. In 1934, Parker Brothers rejected Charles Darrow's game because they said it had 52 design flaws and would never sell. Darrow didn't give up, and today Monopoly is the world's best-selling board game. You will never get bored playing any of the games in this section!

Bottle Cap Checkers

—KENYA—

Checkers is a great board game that is easy to play. The object of the game is to advance your playing pieces across the board to capture your opponent's pieces. In this "war" game, you must use different strategies to win.

The ancient Egyptians, who may have invented checkers, enjoyed playing the game as early as 200 B.C. They used circular objects made from ivory and jade as playing pieces. Carved roof tiles served as game boards. The Egyptians became so fascinated by the game that they decorated their walls and floors with checkerboard designs. During the twelfth century, people in Spain and France played this game, but called it Draughts (pronounced drafts). The game was known by this name in most of Europe. It became so popular that a book was published about it in 1547 in Spain. Today, millions of people around the world, young and old alike, play checkers. There are many variations of checkers. Players in Belgium, France, Russia, the Netherlands, Canada, and Australia use a 100-square board, but in the United States, Great Britain, and Ireland a standard 64-square board is used.

When you play Bottle Cap Checkers, you won't need to go out and buy anything, since it is a snap to make from materials you have around your house. Kids in Kenya make and play Bottle Cap Checkers by drawing the 64-square board on the ground using a stick and by collecting bottle caps to use as playing pieces. Follow the rules below and you'll be a champ in no time.

Game HISTORY

Throughout history, famous people have loved playing checkers. Plato, the Greek philosopher, spoke about the game during many of his **orations** (formal speeches). Ulysses S. Grant, Civil War general and eighteenth President of the United States (from 1869–77), used the game to help sharpen his mental skills for military strategies. He claimed it helped make him successful. Checkers even has its own Hall of Fame. It's located in Petal, Mississippi, in the southern United States.

Bottle Cap Checkers

Players: *2*

Object of the game:

To block your opponent's bottle caps from reaching your side of the board, or to capture all of your opponent's bottle caps.

Here's What You Need

- ☐ 1 16 × 16 inch (40.5 × 40.5 cm) piece of cardboard or oak tag
- ☐ pencil
- ☐ ruler
- ☐ 1 permanent marker or crayon, any dark color
- ☐ 24 bottle caps (12 of one style, such as plastic, and 12 of a different style, such as metal, or 12 of one color and 12 of another color)

Here's What You Do

1 Draw 7 vertical lines that measure 2 inches (5 cm) apart and draw 7 horizontal lines that measure 2 inches (5 cm) apart on the piece of cardboard. There will be 8 squares across the top of the board and 8 squares down the side of the board for a total of 64 squares.

2 Use the marker or crayon to color in the second bottom right square. Now color every other square on the board until all are colored as shown below. Leave the other squares uncolored.

3 Each player takes 12 of the same kind of bottle caps. Place the board in between the two players, then the players put their bottle caps on only the colored squares on their side of the board, starting with the bottom row.

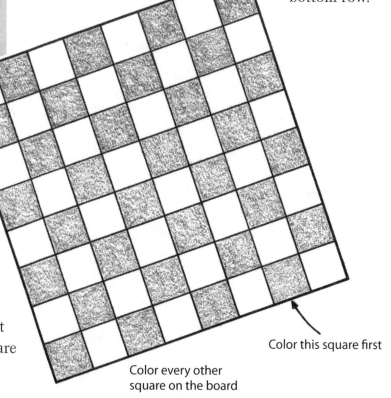

Color this square first

Color every other square on the board

a. Bottle caps can move on colored squares only.

b. Bottle caps can move only diagonally.

c. Bottle caps can be moved only one space at a time.

d. If a player is able to capture the opponent's bottle cap, the player must make that move before making any other move. The player captures his or her opponent's bottle cap by jumping his or her bottle cap over the opponent's bottle cap as shown below.

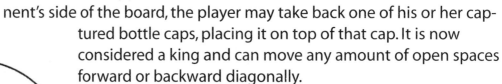

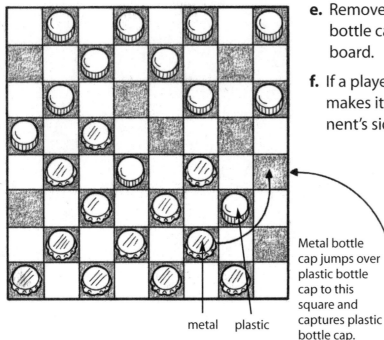

e. Remove all captured bottle caps from the board.

f. If a player's bottle cap makes it to the opponent's side of the board, the player may take back one of his or her captured bottle caps, placing it on top of that cap. It is now considered a king and can move any amount of open spaces forward or backward diagonally.

metal   plastic

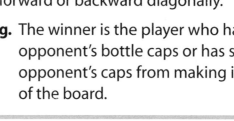

Metal bottle cap jumps over plastic bottle cap to this square and captures plastic bottle cap.

g. The winner is the player who has captured all of his or her opponent's bottle caps or has successfully blocked the opponent's caps from making it to the other player's side of the board.

4 The player with the darker colored bottle caps goes first. May the best player win!

Chess

Chess is another war game that involves strategically moving game pieces that are ranked **hierarchically** (whereby some are more important and powerful than others), including pawns, knights, bishops, rooks, a queen, and a king, to capture your opponent's pieces or block your opponent's pieces from moving. It is believed the earliest test form of this game originated in India around A.D. 600, and from there spread to Persia, Spain, France, other parts of Europe, and the British Isles. Each culture adapted the game slightly. The game became so popular that by the fifteenth century, some players began playing as professionals. The first international tournament, held in London, England, took place in 1851. Since then, chess tournaments have been held all around the world. In Myanmar, three of the chess pieces are different: Instead of a queen, there is a chief of staff, an elephant replaces the bishop, and a chariot replaces the rook.

Mühle

If you like playing Tic-tac-toe, you'll love the German game, Mühle (pronounced MUE-leh). Tic-tac-toe is based on Mühle. This type of game is called an alignment game because the object is to get some of your pieces lined up in a row on the game board.

The ancient Egyptians played a form of Tic-tac-toe. Game boards, made from Egyptian roof tiles, have been found in the ruins of temples near the pyramids. The **Vikings** (Norwegian explorers who lived from A.D. 700 to A.D. 1000) played this game during their long sea voyages to help pass the time. During the fourteenth century, English noblemen played this game outside using servants and children as game pieces and trimmed hedges as the game board. William

Shakespeare wrote about Nine Men's Morris in his play *A Midsummer Night's Dream.* Today, the game is still as popular as it was in ancient times.

Mühle is easy to make and play, but requires some strategy. You have to position your playing pieces, usually stones, on the game board to create a line of three stones. This line is called a "mill," which is what Mühle means. Once you have created your mill, you may capture one of your opponent's stones. Of course, your opponent can do the same to you so you, have to think about where to place your stones.

Mühle

Players: 2

Object of the game:

To block your opponent so that he or she can no longer move any stones, or to capture all your opponent's stones except for two.

Here's What You Need

- [ ] 1 17 × 17 inch (43 × 43 cm) piece of cardboard or oak tag
- [ ] pencil
- [ ] ruler
- [ ] 18 stones
- [ ] permanent marker, any dark color

Here's What You Do

1 Draw 3 squares on the cardboard, decreasing in size. The first square measures 1 inch (2.5 cm) in from each side of the board. The second square measures 2 inches (5 cm) in from each side of the first square. The third

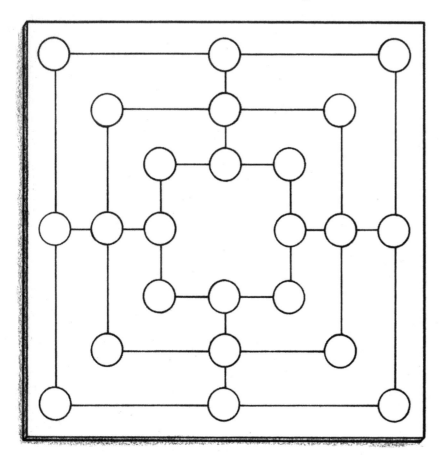

square measures 2 inches (5 cm) in from each side of the second square. After you have drawn the squares, draw 4 lines, one on each side of the board, starting at the first square and ending at the smaller square. Draw 24 circles on the lines of each square as shown here.

2 Divide the stones so that each player has nine. One player must mark his or her stones using the marker. This way, each player will be able to recognize his or her stones.

3 Decide who goes first. The first player places one of his or her stones on any circle on the game board. The opponent does the same. This continues until all the stones have been placed. Remember that stones can be placed only on the circles.

4 While the stones are being placed on the circles, it is important to try to create a "mill" by lining up three stones in a row. The mill must be created on circles that are connected by lines, so no diagonal mills are allowed. If a player creates a mill, he or she may take one of the opponent's stones from the board. The player may not take a stone from his or her opponent's mill unless there are no other stones to take, as shown on page 85.

5 Continue playing by moving the stones along the lines and into circles to try to create mills. Players may move only one space at a time to **adjacent** (next to each other) circles. No diagonal moves are allowed. Jumping an opponent's stone is not allowed. The object is to try to create mills so a player can remove and keep an opponent's stone.

6 Near the end of the game, if one player has only three stones left on the board, that player may move one of his or her stones to any circle. It does not have to be an adjacent circle. The game ends when a player can no longer move any stones or when a player has only two stones left.

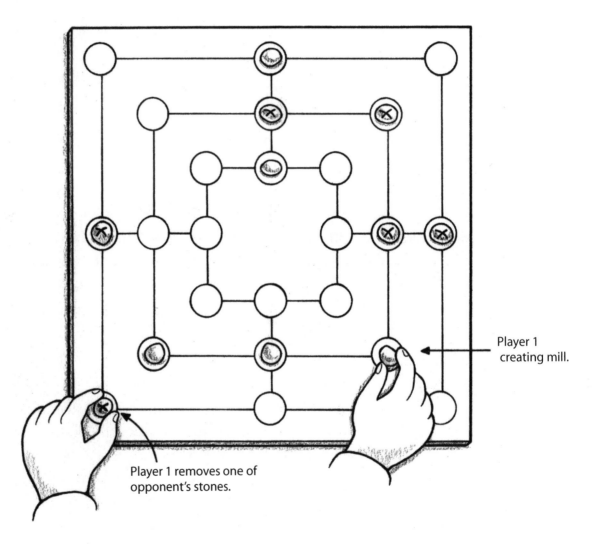

Player 1 creating mill.

Player 1 removes one of opponent's stones.

Culture Link

Go

Another type of alignment game, called Go, is played in Japan. It is also played with stones on a board. The surface of the 19×19 inch (48×48 cm) board is a **grid** (a pattern of horizontal and vertical lines that forms squares). Players each get 180 stones and take turns placing the stones at the **intersections** (places where two lines cross) of the lines. The object of the game is to form rows of stones completely surrounding your opponent's stones. Once a stone is placed on the board, it stays put. You must outsmart your opponent and try to surround his or her stones as they are being placed on the board. Go is an ancient game that may have been played in Japan as early as the sixth century A.D. The **aristocracy** (the privileged upper class) first played the game, but soon **Buddhist** (one who follows the teachings of Buddha) and **Shinto** (native Japanese religion honoring nature spirits and ancestors) clergy and even **samurai** (a member of the Japanese military) warriors played Go. The ancient Chinese and Koreans played this game as well.

Senet

-ANCiENT EGYPT-

The board game Senet is considered a racing game because players have to move, or race, their game pieces around the board until all pieces either exit the game, or get to the winning space. Most racing board games use some type of game piece, often called a pawn, and dice, which are thrown to determine how many spaces the pawns will move around the board. This ancient game was popular in Egypt from about 3000 B.C. to A.D. 400. Archeologists have found game boards in tombs and paintings of Senet games on the walls of tombs. Pawns consisted of triangular- or cone-shaped pieces for one player and circular, flat pieces for the other player. Instead of counting with dice, the Egyptians used sticks that were painted black on one side and white on the other. Eventually, knucklebones were used as dice. Senet was the earliest form of backgammon, a popular game played from ancient times through today.

Racing board games come in all shapes and sizes. Mancala is a board game that has been around for about 7,000 years and is played all over Africa. It might possibly be the oldest game in the world. In Arabic, the word *mancala* means "to transfer." The game is played by moving or transferring game pieces from one shallow bin in the game board to another.

Game HISTORY

Using dice in games dates back to almost 5000 B.C. Archeologists have found early versions of the racing game backgammon and dice dating back to 3000 B.C. in Babylon. Early dice were made of clay, stone, wood, and ivory. These early dice had irregular shapes and tended to favor one side over the others. When dice were used for religious purposes, this irregular shape didn't matter, but when used for **gambling** (betting on a game of chance), it mattered a lot. One of the earliest regularly shaped die, made of pottery, was found in Iraq dating back to 3000 B.C.

The *Maori* (pronounced MAU-ree), the native people of New Zealand, have played the traditional board game, *Mu-Torere,* for hundreds of years. Originally, the game board was scratched on the ground, but eventually the boards were carved into wood. The object of this game is to block your opponent from moving, or racing, around the game board. Pachisi (also known as Parcheesi or Twenty-Five), the national game of India, dates back to the sixth century. Pachisi means twenty-five in Hindi and it is used for this game because this is the highest roll on the dice. The object is to be the first to make it around the + -shaped board to the center square.

You can play Senet just as the ancient Egyptians did. There are several versions. This one is based on one of the earlier versions of Senet.

Senet

Players: *2*

Object of the game:

To be the first player to move all your game pieces off the board.

Here's What You Need

- [ ] 1 6 × 20 inch (15 × 51 cm) piece of cardboard or oak tag
- [ ] pencil
- [ ] ruler
- [ ] scissors
- [ ] permanent black marker
- [ ] 4 craft sticks (or Popsicle sticks)
- [ ] 14 pawns (7 of one small object and 7 of another. Use buttons, coins, paper clips, or any other small object.)

Here's What You Do

1 Using the marker, draw two horizontal lines lengthwise on the cardboard spaced 2 inches (5 cm) apart. Then draw 9 vertical lines spaced 2 inches (5 cm) apart, as shown. This is the Senet board.

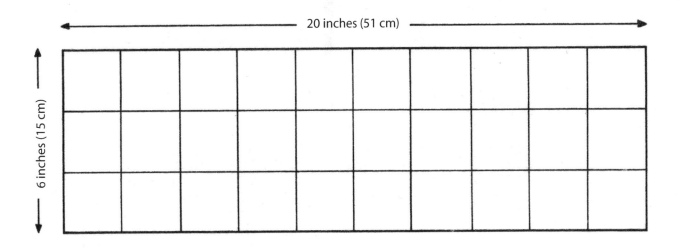

20 inches (51 cm)

6 inches (15 cm)

2 Draw the five Egyptian symbols shown here in the spaces on the Senet board.

3 Using the black marker, color one side of each craft stick. Set aside until the ink dries. The uncolored side is considered white.

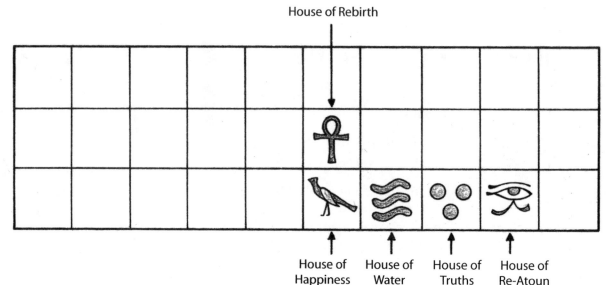

House of Rebirth

House of Happiness   House of Water   House of Truths   House of Re-Atoun

4 Divide the pawns between the two players. Each player should have seven objects. Remember, all your objects should be alike, such as all pennies, and your friend's objects must all be the same, such as all bottle caps.

5 Place the pawns on the Senet board starting at the top row, left side. Each player's pawns must alternate as shown here.

6 The craft sticks are your dice. Here's how to read them.

a. One white side up = 1 move
b. Two white sides up = 2 moves
c. Three white sides up = 3 moves
d. Four white sides up = 4 moves
e. Four black sides up = 6 moves

7 Now you are ready to begin. The first player to roll a 1 goes first. Have fun, but watch out for the House of Waters!

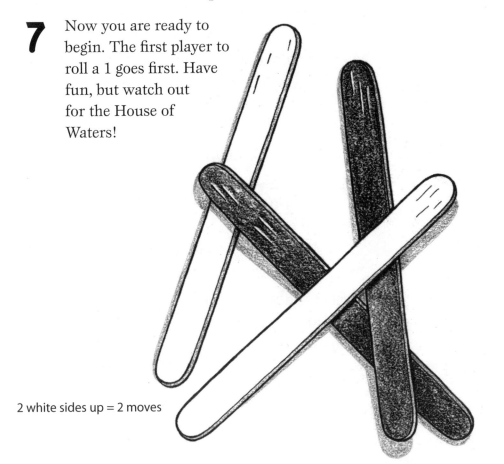

2 white sides up = 2 moves

game rules

a. Players need to toss or drop the sticks to determine how many spaces to move their pawns.

b. Players move their pawns around the board in this order: top row from left to right, middle row from right to left, bottom row from left to right until pawns exit the game at the bottom right.

c. If a player throws a 1, 4, or 6, he or she gets another turn.

d. A player can't land on a space already occupied by one of his or her pawns. You must choose a different pawn to move. If you can't move any pawns at all, you skip your turn.

e. If a player lands on an opponent's space, the player "bumps" the opponent back to the player's original space. But a player cannot "bump" an opponent's pawn if the opponent has two or more pawns in a row. The player must choose a different pawn to move.

f. A player cannot pass the opponent if the opponent has three or more pawns in a row. This is considered a block. The player must move a different pawn. However, a player may pass his or her pawns, or the opponent's pawns, as long as the player does not pass a block.

g. A player may not move a pawn off the board until all his or her pawns are off the first row.

h. The House of Rebirth is a safe space. A player can't bump or be bumped when on this space.

i. The House of Water is a bad space. If a player lands here he or she must go back to the House of Rebirth space. If that space is occupied, the player must go back to the starting space, first square, top left.

j. The House of Happiness is a safe space and players must stop there no matter what they roll on the dice.

k. The House of Truths is a safe space and if a player lands here, the player must roll a 3 to exit the board.

l. The House of Re-Atoun is a safe space and if a player lands here, the player must roll a 2 to exit the board.

m. To exit from the last space, you must roll a 1.

Culture Link

Chinese Checkers

Did you know that Chinese Checkers did not come from China? This racing game is based on the game Halma, which originated in England and other parts of Europe in 1880. The two games are similar in that a person must move his or her pieces, usually marbles, from one corner of the board to the opposite corner of the board. But the game boards look different. The Halma game board is a square and the Chinese Checkers game board is shaped like a six-pointed star. Chinese Checkers became popular in America in the 1930s. Today, it is played all around the world.

PART SIX

Make Terrific Toys

Children have been playing with toys since before recorded history. Early Roman dolls made from a woven material have been found that are more than 2,000 years old. Prehistoric people used wood, clay, stone, grasses, and other natural materials to make dolls and other toys. Through the ages, children have played with yo-yos, pull toys, doll houses, spinning tops, toy soldiers, puppets, kites, and windmills, just to name a few. Mechanical toys with movable parts have also been around for a long time. One favorite of ancient Greece was a wooden dove with flapping wings. Cultural folk toys, often passed down through the generations, have entertained kids for centuries. Rocking horses, pop guns, ball-and-cup, and hoop-and-stick are just a few.

Today, people from all cultures continue to make toys. The Inuit from Alaska and Canada make a yo-yo with a string and two balls made from sealskin. It takes a lot of skill to swing the balls in opposite directions. In Yugoslavia, young children actually learn toy-making in school. Yugoslavians believe it is important for kids to learn to make their own playthings. Dolls are a favorite toy to make and are made from wood, wire, wooden spoons, cloth, fur, and cardboard. In this section, you will create your own totally terrific toys.

Galimoto

—MALAWI—

In Malawi, Cameroon, and other African countries, children enjoy making toys out of old wire, sticks, and other materials they find in their villages. These toys are called *galimoto* (GAL-lee-moh-toh), which means "motorcar" in the Malawi language. But cars aren't the only recycled toys kids make in Malawi. Helicopters, trucks, bikes, trains, and buses are just a few of the things. Sometimes the child attaches a stick to the toy to push it along the ground.

Construction toy-making began a long time ago. More than 2,000 years ago, the Romans made toys with wheels of clay. One favorite was a clay bird. The pre-Columbian Maya also made toys on wheels, though they never used the wheel for their own transportation—just for toys. Today, children make all kinds of fabulous creations with parts such as Legos, K'nex, and Robotix.

You can make your own galimoto out of pipe cleaners. Since your galimoto will be your own creation, you can design it any way you'd like. Here are some drawings of different galimoto that might help you get some ideas before you create your own.

Here's What You Need

- 1 8^1/$_2$ × 11 inch (21.5 × 28 cm) sheet of paper
- pencil
- about 50 pipe cleaners (in different colors)
- scissors

Game HISTORY

Erector Set

As a young boy in the late 1800s, A. C. Gilbert loved playing with homemade toys and performing magic tricks for his friends. As an adult, he worked as a magician to help pay his tuition to medical school. But instead of becoming a doctor, he went into the toy business and created a toy that he believed would educate as well as entertain children: the Erector set. It was a construction kit filled with metal beams, bolts, screws, pulleys, gears, and even engines. Kids would spend hours constructing bridges, skyscrapers, cars, and even a walking robot. The kits became more elaborate, and began to include enough parts for kids to construct power plants and an entire amusement park with a working Ferris wheel. Gilbert went on to manufacture model trains, chemistry sets, and glass-blowing kits, but the Erector set was one of the most popular toys of its time.

safety alert

The tips of pipe cleaners can be sharp. Be careful when twisting the ends together. You may want to bend the tips back so the sharp parts do not stick out.

Twist tip of small piece around wheel edge for spoke

Car frame

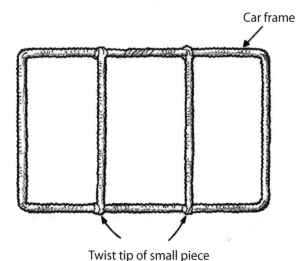

Twist tip of small piece around frame for supports

Here's What You Do

1 Decide what you want your galimoto to be, such as a car, a truck, or a helicopter, then sketch your galimoto on paper. Be sure to keep it simple.

2 Using the pipe cleaners, start to create your galimoto. You may need to cut the pipe cleaners to make the wheels or other small parts of your car or truck. To make a wheel, bend a piece of pipe cleaner into a circle and twist the ends of the pipe cleaner together. To make the spokes of the wheel, use a small piece of pipe cleaner, twist one end around one edge of the wheel and twist the other end around the opposite edge of the

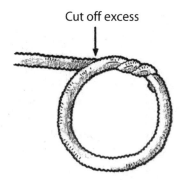

Cut off excess

Twist pipe cleaner tip around edge of circle to form wheel

wheel. To hold the frame of your car together, use support pipe cleaners along the bottom of the car frame.

3 Follow the design you drew to finish your galimoto, but don't worry if it comes out a little different from your design. Galimoto tend to take on a life of their own during creation. Everyone's galimoto will look unique.

Model Cars

In the 1940s, children in America played with cars that they assembled from balsa wood. Model car kits, sold in hardware, toy, and department stores, contained all the parts needed for the child to assemble the car. Companies such as Monogram, Revell, and Aluminum Model Toys manufactured these kits, but none of the models represented cars from that time period. The models were replicas of cars from the 1920s, race cars, or futuristic cars. That all changed in the late 1940s when Aluminum Model Toys made promotional model cars, or promos, for car dealers to use when customers wanted to buy a car. These

promos were made from aluminum and were painted in the colors offered by the dealer. The dealer gave out the model cars to families who either test drove or bought a car. Another change occurred with the invention of the plastic mold injection method. Using this method, the parts for these promos could be molded in plastic in the colors offered by the dealer, eliminating the need to paint the aluminum parts. This all but eliminated the need for aluminum so the company changed its name to AMT (an acronym for Aluminum Model Toys). It wasn't long before the idea to package these model car kits for kids, collectors, and hobbyists took hold. This was also the first time that replicas of present-day cars were used. Today kids can make many different types and styles of cars using model car kits.

Jumping Jack

—UNITED STATES—

Some of the earliest prehistoric puppets, consisting of jointed skulls and masks with hinges, were used in religious ceremonies. Later, bodies were added to the skulls and masks and may have been attached to a stick or string. The Egyptians had stringed puppets in the second century B.C., while puppet theaters became popular in ancient Greece and India.

Marionettes are puppets that are maneuvered by strings from above. The movement of their arms, legs, and heads makes them seem lifelike. During a puppet show, the puppeteer hides behind the stage scenery, completely out of the audience's view. It is easier to operate marionettes than hand puppets because the puppeteer gets to stand, using gravity to his or her advantage, while the hand puppet operator must hold up his or her arms for long periods of time. Marionette performances are often done in a small opera house, where people can enjoy operas by Mozart, Rossini, Offenbach, and other famous composers. One of the most famous marionette theaters, the Salzburg Marionette Theater, in the European country of Austria, is a delight to visit. You might see an opera, operetta, or ballet all performed by marionettes. The performances are so exciting that you may forget you are watching puppets.

The art of puppetry has evolved over the years to include many different types, such as marionettes, hand puppets, finger puppets, dancing puppets, paper puppets, rod puppets, shadow puppets, miniature puppets, and jumping jacks. Jumping jacks are hundreds of years old and found in many cultures. It is believed that this toy came from France and was originally made for adults. The French name for these puppets is *Le Pantin* (leuh pau-tah). In Germany, the jumping jack is called *Hampelmann* and artists who make them paint on lederhosen, the traditional clothing of Germany.

A jumping jack is a puppet with movable arms and legs. There is a string at the top of the puppet used for holding the puppet in the air and another string hanging from the bottom for making the arms and legs move up and down. Jumping jacks are made from different materials, but wood is one of the most popular because it is durable. Jumping jacks can represent people, animals, and nursery-rhyme characters. People who live in the region surrounding the Appalachian Mountains make many folk toys by hand. Each toy has its own history, which is passed down through generations by word-of-mouth. While the jumping jack did not originate in Appalachia, it has become a favorite toy of the children who live there.

You can make a simple jumping jack in the style of the Appalachian carved wooden puppets, but you will use oak tag instead of wood. Many of these jumping jacks depict simple country life. Folk-art puppets and toys are made to work without the use of batteries or electricity. Any part that moves does so because of how it's put together. You will have a basic pattern to use for your jumping jack, but you can make it into any character you wish.

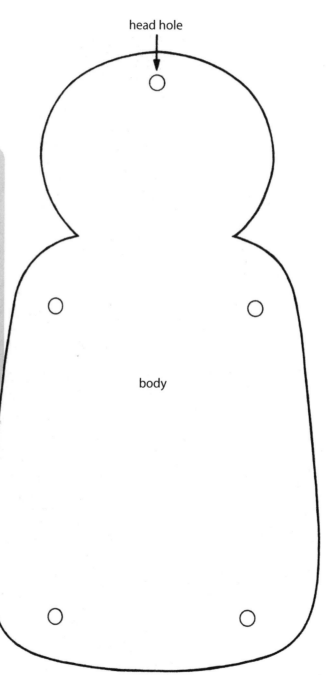

head hole

body

Here's What You Need

- [ ] a few sheets of tracing paper
- [ ] pencil
- [ ] scissors
- [ ] 1 12 × 12 inch (30 × 30 cm) piece of poster board, such as oak tag
- [ ] hole punch (optional)
- [ ] permanent markers in a variety of colors
- [ ] glue stick
- [ ] scraps of material such as felt, fur, calico, or whatever you have around the house
- [ ] 4 brass paper fasteners
- [ ] string (thin string works better)
- [ ] small plastic ring, old button, or other small object that will be used as a handle
- [ ] adult helper

Here's What You Do

1 Place the tracing paper over the pattern shown here and, using the pencil, trace the body shape and arms and legs.

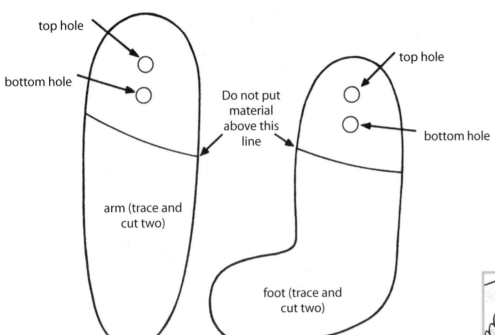

top hole

bottom hole

Do not put material above this line

arm (trace and cut two)

top hole

bottom hole

foot (trace and cut two)

4 Use the markers and material scraps to decorate your jumping jack. You can use the material scraps for clothes. Try not to cover up the holes on the body, but if you do, **HAVE AN ADULT** poke the scissors through the material. Do not put any material or decorations above the lines on the arms and legs. Let the glue dry.

5 Assemble the jumping jack by placing the arms and legs behind the body. Push the brass fasteners through the holes in the body, then through the *bottom* holes in the arms and legs. Bend the ends of the fasteners as shown. (Note: Make sure the fasteners are not attached *too* tightly. The arms and legs should be able to move easily.)

2 Cut out the traced pieces and place them on the oak tag. Hold down one at a time and trace the shape onto the oak tag. Do this for all of the shapes.

3 **HAVE AN ADULT** help you carefully poke the pointed end of the scissors through the circles on the shapes or use the hole punch. Cut out all the shapes.

back of body

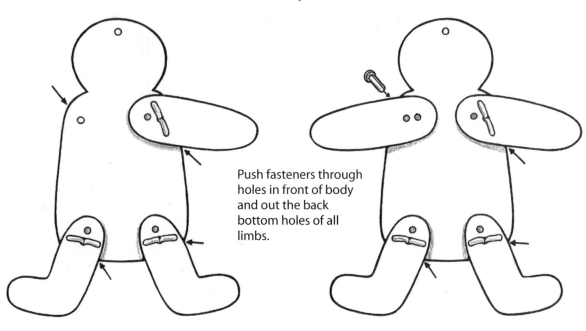

Push fasteners through holes in front of body and out the back bottom holes of all limbs.

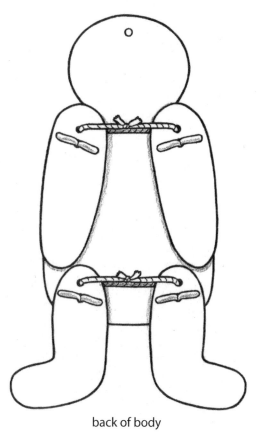

Place string through top holes of all limbs and secure with knot.

back of body

6 Insert a piece of string first through the top holes in the arms. *The arms must be hanging down against the sides of the body.* Tie the string in a tight knot. The arms will want to move away from the body as you tie the knot. Have someone hold them in place if this happens. Repeat this step for the legs, putting the string through the top holes in the legs. *The legs must hang straight down as you tie the knot.* If they move, have someone hold them in place as you tie the knot. Cut off any excess string.

7 Attach a 24-inch (61 cm) piece of string at the center point of the arms' string and then at the center point of the legs' string, letting the string hang down about 6 inches (15 cm) from the bottom of the body. The arms and legs must hang straight down as you tie the knot. Cut off any excess string. Tie the ring to the end of the string.

8 Attach a 12-inch (30-cm) piece of string to the hole in the head. Tie the ends in a tight knot.

Long string is attached to arm string and leg string with a knot.

9 Pull on the bottom string to move the jumping jack's arms and legs.

Water Puppets

Professional puppeteers in Vietnam stage beautiful performances with water puppets. This art dates back to the tenth century when farmers used them to celebrate harvests. The farmers always performed the show on a bamboo stage that was built in a pond. Elaborate village scenery was made and attached to wires strung on stakes. The puppets, attached to long bamboo poles, moved through the water with the help of the farmer, who hid behind a rattan curtain while standing in waist-deep water. Learning this unique form of puppetry is a skill passed down from generation to generation. It is not easy because the puppeteer's hands, which operate the puppet, are underwater. The painted wooden puppets can be as tall as 3 feet (1 m). The body of the puppet is usually above the water, but sometimes dips down under the water and back up again. Music accompanying the show introduces the theme of the performance. A display of fireworks takes place after the performance.

Bilboquet

A popular toy in Europe from the sixteenth through the eighteenth centuries was the *bilboquet* (pronounced beel-boh-kay). The toy consisted of a ball attached to a string, which was then attached to a cup. The object of the game was to swing or jerk the ball up into the air and then get the ball to land in the cup. It sounds easy, but it took practice and great eye-hand coordination to figure out just how to swing the ball. Everyone from royalty to peasants enjoyed this toy. Even the king of France, Henri III, loved playing the game. Craftsmen hand-carved these toys from wood, and for a special occasion the artist might carve one from ivory. Many of the *bilboquet* were painted.

Cup-and-ball toys were played by the ancient Greeks and Romans. Today, in Mexico and South America, it is called *balero* (pronounced bah-LEH-doh), and there, the ball does not have a round shape, but is drum-shaped. This requires a different range of swinging motions from the user. The Inuit have made a version of this toy for years from carved bones. Players try to get a target bone, which is attached to a string and looks like a small spear, into a catcher bone, which has an opening and looks like a tube. Hand-carved cup and ball games were played by the **Amish** (a religious group who came to America in the 1700s from Germany and France), people from Appalachia, and by the pioneer children in America in the 1800s.

These toys are easy to make and will give you and your friends hours of fun. This is a great way to practice your eye–hand coordination skills.

Here's What You Need

- [ ] newspaper
- [ ] string
- [ ] scissors
- [ ] masking tape
- [ ] 1 plastic 6–8 ounce (175–250 ml) cup with a rim diameter of about 3 inches (8 cm)
- [ ] pencil

Here's What You Do

1 Take about $^1/_2$ sheet of newspaper and roll it up into a ball with a diameter of about 2 inches (5 cm). If your paper ball is larger, unroll it and tear off some of the newspaper. Then roll it into a ball again and measure.

2 Cut a piece of string about 36 inches (91 cm) long. Tie one end around the paper ball and secure it with a tight knot. Cover the ball with the masking tape. You don't need a lot of tape, just enough so that the paper won't unroll. You will cover part of the string as well, but leave the one end of the string free.

3 You can tie the loose end of the string around the base of the cup and secure it with a tight knot, or you can simply tape the end of the loose string to the bottom of the cup. See illustration on page 108.

4 Measure $1^1/_2$ inches (4 cm) from the bottom of the cup and mark the spot with the pencil. Starting at the rim of the cup, cut down to the mark, then cut around the cup to cut off the top part of the cup. Test out your ball-and-cup toy to see if you can get the ball in the cup.

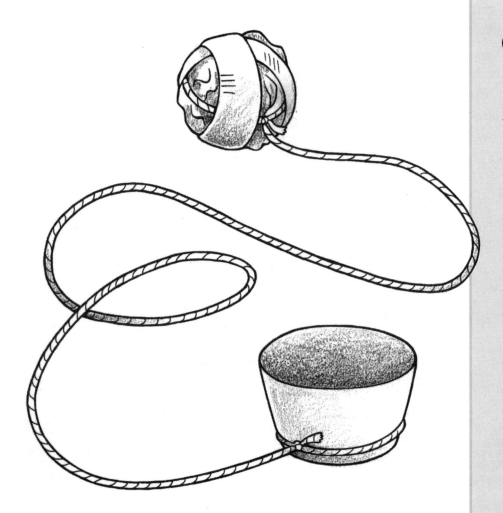

Culture Link

The Dreidel

The dreidel is a type of spinning top. Spinning tops have been found in almost all cultures. The earliest top may have been a nut that prehistoric man twirled between his fingers. There are many different types of tops. Plunger tops have a handle that causes the top to spin when it is pumped up and down. Finger tops are simply twirled between the thumb and fingers. Flip tops actually flip over when you spin them. The peg top has a string wound around it. When it is thrown and released from the string, it spins. The dreidel, which dates back 2,000 years, is a finger top and is used by Jewish children during Hanukkah to play the dreidel game. The four Hebrew letters on the dreidel determine if the player will lose all of his or her tokens, miss a turn, put a token in the pot, or take half the pot.

Glossary

adjacent   Next to.

agility   The ability to move quickly.

Amish   A religious group who came to America in the 1700s from Germany and France.

archipelago   A large group of islands.

aristocracy   The privileged upper class.

billiards   A game in which a ball, called a cue, is used to hit three hard balls against one another or against the sides of a rectangular table.

Buddhist   One who follows the teachings of Buddha.

cane   The flexible stem of certain bamboo.

Civil War   The war between the Northern Union and the Southern Confederacy, from 1861 to 1865.

circumference   The distance around a circle.

deal   To give or hand out.

diagram   A drawing to show how something works.

divination   Fortune-telling.

gambling   Betting on a game of chance.

Great Depression   A time of great economic difficulty in the United States.

grid   A pattern of horizontal and vertical lines that forms squares.

gum   A sticky plant substance.

hierarchically   A ranking of people more important and powerful than others.

Hispaniola   An island in the Caribbean made up of the nations of Haiti and the Dominican Republic.

intersection   A place where two lines cross.

lottery   A contest in which winners are selected in a random drawing.

maize   Corn.

marker   An object used as a game piece.

matte   A flat or unshiny finish.

occult   Relating to the supernatural.

orations   Formal speeches.

pair   Two items.

papyrus   A tall, aquatic grasslike plant from northern Africa.

Roman Forum   The great center of Rome where meetings took place.

samurai   A member of the Japanese military.

Shinto   A native Japanese religion honoring nature spirits and ancestors.

sinew   A tendon or fibrous tissue that connects muscle to bone.

Yupik   The native peoples of western Alaska and northeast Russia.

Vikings   Norwegian explorers who lived from A.D. 700 to A.D. 1000.

PUZZLE ANSWERS

Answer to riddle on page 8: a snail.

Answer to tangram puzzles on page 12:

index